*"As you read through the pages of this book,
you will be touched by Mr. McDonald's unique perspective on
fatherhood. May God use Gavin's words as an encouragement
for his daughter, Kinley, as well as the rest of us to believe
in the depth of our Heavenly Father's love!"*
—Pastor Trent Morgan
Grace Community Church; Salem, MO

*"Gavin's heart for his family and God is so evident
in his work that it will touch every reader to their core.
He provides brilliant, Godly insight into raising Christian
children in a heartwarming, yet practical manner. I truly believe
that every person, whether single, married, or married
with children can learn from "Raise Her Up"
and I wholeheartedly recommend it.*
—Pastor Matthew Barnett
Founder of The Dream Center; Los Angeles, CA

Raise Her Up

Copyright © 2015 Gavin McDonald. All rights reserved.

No rights claimed for public domain material, all rights reserved. No parts of this publication may be reproduced, stored in any retrieval system, or transmitted in any form or by any means, electronic, mechanical, recording, or otherwise, without the prior written permission of the author. This book is a work of fiction. Names, characters, places, and incidents either are products of the author's imagination or are used fictitiously. Any resemblance to actual events or locales or persons, living or dead, is entirely coincidental. Violations may be subject to civil or criminal penalties.

Library of Congress Control Number: 2015956055

ISBN: 978-1-63308-186-4 Hardback
              978-1-63308-187-1 Paperback
              978-1-63308-188-8 Digital

Interior and Cover Design by R'tor John D. Maghuyop

1028 S Bishop Avenue, Dept. 178
Rolla, MO 65401

Printed in United States of America

GAVIN McDONALD

RAISE HER UP

CHALFANT ECKERT
PUBLISHING

To Kinley Marie McDonald
My Punkin, My Princess, My Joy

And to my beautiful wife Kylie
Without you, this wouldn't have been possible…literally.

TABLE OF CONTENTS

Acknowledgements 9

Introduction 11

Part 1:   The Waiting Game 15

Part 2:   The Arrival 29

Part 3:   Going Home 37

Part 4:   The Holidays 43

Part 5:   A Brand New Year 51

Part 6:   My Spring Chicken 75

Part 7:   So Many Plans 89

Part 8:   Growing So Fast 103

Part 9:   My May Flower 113

Part 10: My Summertime Sweetie 127

Part 11: My Autumn Angel 157

Part 12: Closing 179

ACKNOWLEDGEMENTS

My wife, Kylie. You've put up with this ADHD, OCD, man-child for much longer than anyone ever would have expected! Thank you for being a mother that loves her child unconditionally. You are my source of enduring strength and affection. Thank you for choosing me to experience this journey alongside. I love you deeply.

My dad. You've hand crafted the blueprint on what an amazing father looks like. You've taught me patience, godliness, kindness, and everything else in between. I've lived every day in an attempt to make you proud, and you'll forever be my greatest hero. I love you endlessly.

My mother. You prayed for me before I was born. You've prayed for me every day since. If I had a message that I desperately needed to make sure God heard, you would be the one I'd ask to deliver it. The foundation of Jesus' love that you've instilled in my spirit has made me the man I am today. I know God personally, and it's all because of you. I love you more.

My sister, Christy. Sis, you've always been the one I could lean on when my world seemed to be crashing down around me. Thank you for the tough love you've shown many times over the phone after my many failures in life. No one else could rip me apart the way you could, and I would still know how much you cared for me. You're such an amazing person, because you've become so many in one: you have Mom's heart, Grandma Koogler's spirit, and Grandma McDonald's laughter. I love you truly.

My brother Nathan. No matter the situation, you were always the voice of reason. I could spill out all my problems while you listen, and

ACKNOWLEDGEMENTS

then you'd give me the practical way to fix it. Not words I just needed to hear, or simple phrases like, "I'll pray for you." No, you were always the meat and potatoes, and the "here's what you should do" kind of brother. More times than not, you were the only one who would never judge me. You would take my failures and love me still. I love you, bro.

To my nieces Natalie, Neely, and Ayla. And to my nephews Landon, Noah, Jake, and Easton. To my all my aunts, uncles, cousins, friends, pastors, church family, and co-workers. Every one of you has made an impression on my life that will echo in eternity. I love you all.

And to my forever father. There are not enough letters on this keyboard to adequately express my love and affection. You've taken a broken man that's crushed your heart constantly, and proven that mercy is the greatest gift ever given. If I had nothing in this world, I would still have you. From the deepest recesses of my heart, I thank you for this life. You have blessed this sinful man so much more than I have ever deserved, and I will use eternity to praise you. You're my everything, and I'll love you forever.

INTRODUCTION

I am not an author. Though my name may be on the front of this book and I have typed all these words, I could never consider myself an actual author. "Author" is a term for those with intellect, imagination, and skills. I don't consider myself fluent in any of these qualities. This is simply a story.

When my niece Natalie was born, I was overcome with joy and happiness for that little ball of flesh. As I watched the visitors come and go, I was overcome with all the great gifts that were brought to her. The hospital room was filled with flowers, balloons, diapers, bottles, toys, and clothes. I half expected to see the Wise Men show up at any second with gold, frankincense, and myrrh.

As a 16-year-old boy on a minimum wage lifeguard salary, most of my extra cash had to go to Stridex pads, but I desperately wanted to give her something. When you love someone, there is this deep desire to give them things. As I sat contemplating what I could give that would mean more than a box of poop catchers, I decided to write her a letter. I sealed it up, and wrote on the front, "Do not open until February 6th, 2014" – her sixteenth birthday.

We were finally able to open the old, faded letter last year. As I read it to my niece during her birthday party, we were all overcome with emotion. I was barely able to make it through the mere three pages, as tears streamed down my face. It was the greatest gift I've ever given.

Were the words so poetic that I was thereafter referred to as the Shakespeare of my time? Absolutely not! Was the punctuation perfect, the margins all correct, the flow precise, and all the words spelled correctly? Not in the slightest. But no one cared, because the words were

INTRODUCTION

poured onto the page from a young, stupid man that simply wanted the ones he loved to be able to read his heart.

This is what this book is all about. A few weeks before Kinley was born, I realized that the trials we were already facing I would want to remember forever. I intended it to be a couple pages long, simply to let her read on some great occasion later in her life.

A couple months after her arrival, I noticed that this project had gone well beyond a quick letter. As a nurse in the ER, I've seen countless young lives end without notice, well before anyone had anticipated. No one is guaranteed tomorrow. There's no guarantee that I'll be there to teach her how to live, how to treat others, how to pray, and how to grow.

So, I spent her entire first year writing all these thoughts down. I recount the funny times, the first's, all the things I did right and wrong, the struggles of fatherhood, the sad times, and many life lessons I've learned during my 33 years of successes and failures.

But a quick note to reader: For all those reading this book outside of my immediate family, the first few months are actually kind of boring, I admit. Who wants to read about what some random guy bought his wife on Christmas morning, or who came to visit on a certain day? I know I wouldn't! But when I began writing, it wasn't intended to go any further than my close family and friends. So please, stick with it. The second half is filled with inspiration for anyone that has ever been a child or a parent (see what I did there? ... yeah, it's for everyone).

So, again, I'm not an author. I'm simply a father -- a father who has learned a ton of wisdom from his own father and his Heavenly Father and desires to pass it onto a little girl who stole his heart within seconds of her arrival.

The Bible says that if we raise our children in the ways of the Lord, that when they are older, they will not leave it. I may be the best at teaching her how to walk. I may succeed at helping her with algebra, and provide her with excellent financial advice. I may make it to every recital, concert, and play. But all of this is useless if I don't instill in her heart the only thing that really matters: the love of God.

If I fail at everything I attempt for the rest of my life, as long as I raise her up in God, then I've accomplished the only task he requires of me. A Godly father is the only father to be, and I present the same challenge to every father out there.

So look past my grammatical errors, and don't judge me on the possible misspellings. I truly hope you enjoy reading it, and if you don't, my feelings won't be hurt – it wasn't written for you anyway!

Gavin McDonald

PART 1

THE WAITING GAME

October 12, 2014

Last night was the first time since mommy had the stitch placed to keep you baking for a few more weeks, that I left town. I had to DJ a wedding for a co-worker down in Mountain View. As I was in the middle of the reception, I'm sure while playing "Cupid Shuffle" for the gazzilionth time, I got the call. Her back had been hurting terribly over the last couple days, which we shook off as simply a pinched nerve. She had sent me a couple texts during the wedding that it was getting worse. When I answered the phone, I knew something was wrong and told her to just go straight to the ER to make sure everything was okay.

I immediately told the bride that something was wrong, and had to leave. She understood, and I left all my music equipment and lights and ran to my car to get on the road, since I was about 2 hours away from Rolla. I was still an hour and a half from home when mommy's friend Emily called to say that they were flying her to St. Louis. Needless to say, I began to pray fast and drive even faster. I had the speech already memorized in my brain on what I would plea to the cops when they inevitably pulled me over, and it was bitter sweet that I didn't, because it would have been Oscar worthy. Your Mama and Papaw McDonald were down in Joplin, visiting your uncle Nathan when I called to let them know the unfolding situation. Of course, they also got on the road immediately, even with me pleading they didn't need to, as they had more than 5 hours to drive. But you will eventually figure out that their grandkids are their world. It's a good thing you weren't being delivered on some deserted island, because Mema would be trying to use her one good arm to row across the ocean.

I made it to the Rolla hospital just in time to see your Mom for a few minutes before the helicopter crew was to arrive and strap her up for transport. The contractions for roughly 2-3 minutes apart, so everyone was moving pretty fast, as was my increasing heart rate. They were giving her medication to try to stop the contractions, which in turn was making her swell up like the Popeye balloon in the Macy's Parade. They could have probably given her just a tad more, and let her *float* to St. Louis (which I would prefer, having no idea what this little chopper ride is going to cost us). I've never had a stranger moment than when I was speeding down I-44 towards St. Louis and seeing the helicopter that held my wife and unborn baby girl above me disappearing from view.

I made it to St. Louis SSM St. Mary's at about 1:30 in the morning. They were still giving mommy the bloating magnesium IV to help stop the contractions, and began the steroid injections to aid in developing your tiny, young lungs. The doctor came in and decided to remove the stitch, due to it beginning to rip through the cervix. This was the most pain I've ever seen your mom in, and it broke my heart. It was the first time in our lives we were both crying together. Your Mema and Papaw arrived at around 3:00 (after he was lost in downtown St. Louis for an hour). Needless to say, it was an *extremely* long night. They did an ultrasound this morning, which says you are about 5 pounds! This is much more than what we were expecting, which is amazing. It may be a blessing that you're coming early, because at this rate, you might have held the "Biggest Baby Ever Born" title for Guinness. (Not that I would have loved you any less, but mommy's boobies can only put out so much.) It's been a really long night and day, but we expect you at any time so it's hard for me to sleep. On a side note, your nurse is a spitting image of Kathy Bates…look her up.

"The most important thing a father can do for his children is to love their mother."
—Rev. Theodore Hesburgh

October 14, 2014

Well, you're still not here, but that's a good thing. Your mom is proving to be one tough cookie, and the pain and contractions have finally slowed down. They have moved us out of the ICU to the other side of the floor, room 581. Your Mema and Papaw left yesterday to go back home since you're surprisingly still inside. Your Papa Jordan visited yesterday, and is so excited to meet you. They've stopped the magnesium today, thank God. The medicine made your mom very dizzy and weak, plus caused her to have extremely blurry vision. She hated it, and is glad to now be on Procardia, which is pretty much the same medication to stop contractions, but is a pill instead of IV.

Since we knew we would be here a while, I went to the store today to get some groceries. And by groceries, I mean a ton of candy for your mother. I also had to go to Walgreens to buy a radio, since the hospital doesn't have the channel that is showing the National League Championship games! Our beloved Cardinals are back in the hunt for a World Series. We are playing the Giants, but sadly down in the series right now. Hopefully they can pull it out. The Cardinals won the World Series the year I was born (1982), and figured it was only fitting they win it again the year you're born!

THE WAITING GAME

I also went to the laundromat today to wash our clothes. I was only able to grab a couple items before coming up here, so I was out of underwear, which is an emergency. The laundromat was scary and intimidating, and thought I would surely be raped and murdered at any given time. There's a lot of racial tension going on right now in Ferguson, Missouri (just a few blocks north of us actually) from a shooting that killed a young black man by a white police officer a few months back. They've had tons of rioting and looting, so I'm a little nervous to show my very white skin around here right now. But I made it back to the hospital safe and sound (with a little help from the gun being very visual on my hip).

"It is much easier to become a father than to be one."
—Kent Nerburn

October 16, 2014

It's late, but thought I would just write a quick note. Sadly, our Cardinals have lost the NLCS to the stinking Giants. Your mom kept getting mad at me while I was listening to the game on the radio. I got a little upset, of course, and threw the radio, breaking it on the ground. I get into the games a little, as I'm sure you'll find out.

Your mom is doing excellent. I really can NOT believe you're not here yet. Watch you make a fool out of all of us and end up going the full 40 weeks! That would be nuts. A lady came by the room today to let us know that they are doing crafts at 2 o'clock, and that we were welcome to come. Well, of course I drug your mother down there. We ended up making a wreath out of diapers, and decorating it in fall colors. I made a big bow by hand to put it on the top of the wreath, and all the other patients ended up asking me make one for them as well! I'm definitely my father's son. Speaking of your grandparents, they ended up actually showing up during crafts time to surprise us! We got so tickled going down the hall back to our room, when we realized that Papaw was pushing Mema in her wheelchair and I was pushing your mom in hers! We, of course, had to have a couple races (I won).

I have been spending most of my time reading. I'm in the middle of the Left Behind series again. I've read two books in the last two days, and probably will be reading a lot more! Anything I can do to pass the time. It drags like a two legged dog in here.

October 17, 2014

"You have not, because you ask not." I did NOT like our room we were in. It was about the size of a turtle shell, and our view was of the back of the hospital- depressing! So I asked if there was a different room on the other side. Well, Tara the nurse came to our rescue, and got us a different room, so we moved into 860 today. The view is leaps and bounds better! We have Forrest Park to our right, Fontbonne University right in front of us, the hospital fountain below us, and all the trees leaves are changing colors. Plus, the room is bigger, and has actual shelves around the sink. It's no Hilton, but it's perfection when it comes to hospital rooms. I unloaded all our clothes into the shelves, so we wouldn't have to be digging through our bags for clothes every day- a shimmer of normality in our lives right now could do wonders. Your mom thought it was ridiculous when we were packing everything up to move rooms, but now that we're in it, she's (quietly) saying I was right! I win, mark it down.

Mommy has been having a lot more contractions today, so she called the nurse to let the doctors know. She's now 90% effaced and dilated to 2 cm. We keep thinking that you'll be here any day, any minute, but we've now realized that you're going to be stubborn like your mother. Remind me to spank you later.

October 18, 2014

We got outside today! Hallelujah, oh glorious day! This may seem like a small deal to the unknowing reader that's snuggly reading this from the warmth of their own couch, but you would have thought we were walking out onto a beach. It's been such beautiful weather that we decided we needed out of this room, before we ended up killing each other. I found a wheelchair, and heard through the grapevine that there's an outside patio on the top floor. We went up to the 6th, and found the patio. It was magnificent, what I could see of it through the tears welling in my eyes. We can see the Arch off to the east, and most of St. Louis around us.

We stayed out for a while, and then I pushed your mom around the hospital for a little bit. My favorite part was to go really fast, and then let go and run beside her. She didn't think it was NEAR as funny as I did, of course. I also liked to start sprinting with her every time she said she was having a contraction, while yelling "HOT WATER, HOT WATER!!" I find it hilarious every single time.

As you'll find out throughout your life, your father is extremely hyperactive. This has been the hardest thing I've ever had to do, sitting here in this jail cell. I feel like a caged tiger. At times, I wish I had a piece of chalk, to track the days inside on the wall like a death row prisoner. If we go any longer, I see myself burrowing through the wall with a cafeteria spoon, covering up my process with a "Hand Hygiene" poster I've found. So I've had several moments of going crazy, of course. I've used your mom's monitor straps as ties, headbands, ninja weapons, etc. There's also this device on the ceiling that's used for moving obese patients. It's on a rolling track, so I usually go swinging from that a couple times a day, hollering like Tarzan. The same thing always happens: I laugh hysterically, and your mother rolls her eyes at me. That's my life!

Your Aunt Christy, and cousins, Noah and Neely, came to visit today. They had a bible quiz competition in St. Louis, so swung by afterwards. They brought mommy a bag of goodies (as if she needed one more ounce of sweets), and Aunt Christy gave you a Cardinals blanket that she made. You will grow up a die-hard fan, this is a must. Neely would watch you move around in your mom's belly with this look of horror on her face. She kept saying it looked like an alien. Hopefully, you don't come out looking like one. That would be weird, but also kind of cool, I guess.

> *"Someday my children will look fondly on the annoying things I did and see them clearly as evidence of love."*
> —Richelle E. Goodrich

October 21, 2014

We made it 33 weeks! It's crazy to think back to when we were here at 22 weeks, and the doctors telling us that the priority was to make it to 24, and we likely wouldn't make it past 28. God is so good to us, and you have already proven to be a miracle. I love you so much already, and I've never been more excited for anything in my life. I'm literally hurting to see you, to hold you, to love on you. I know you'll come when you're ready, but UGH… I want to have you NOW!

I decided to go home to Rolla today to grab some more clothes and extra stuff from the house. I had to run around and pay some bills, go by work to talk about insurance, pick up mommy's new breast pump, and get my Xbox from the house. I also got a few more books, some scary movies, your mom's face trimmer (heehee), and some extra t-shirts. It was nice to get out and about. The only thing bad about the day is that I missed craft class. Crap. Those poor saps had to settle for subpar, bow-less diaper cakes.

> "Babies are always more trouble than you thought – and more wonderful."
> —Charles Osgood

October 23, 2014

All work and no play makes Dad a dull boy. All work and no play makes Dad a dull boy… I feel like I'm losing my mind! (If you don't get this reference, ask me or go watch The Shining). It was actually a pretty full day. Mommy started having contractions at about 10:00 this morning, and they were roughly 5 minutes apart. They checked her and she was dilated to a 3.

We ended up going back to crafts class today (I again had to drag your mom). We made diaper cakes! We went with the fall theme again, with one of my special bows on top (of course). I almost didn't do it, because I knew I'd end up having to make one for everyone again… And sure enough, I did.

There's a couple other girls that have been here a while as well. One girl is pregnant with boy/girl twins who will make numbers 5 and 6 of kids. The other girl is also pregnant with twins, which will make numbers 6 and 7!

The contractions didn't slow down all day, and ended up coming about every 3 minutes this afternoon. We may be getting closer! They ended up checking her for dilation 4 times, but said she wasn't changing. We have had a new female doctor this week that is really pushing to the possibility of sending us home soon. We are concerned that we'll be discharged and as soon as we get home, mommy will go into labor, we'll end up delivering at Rolla, then you'll have to be shipped to St. Louis. I would rather just stay here as long as we can, and possibly go home closer to 36 weeks, but we shall see.

Your great aunt Bev and uncle Flan surprised us today with a visit. It was great to see them, and have someone to talk to, besides the housekeeping lady. They didn't stay long, but was happy to see them. One day at a time, there Princess! Even though we're so excited to see your face, you just keep on cooking!

"We worry about what a child will become tomorrow, yet we forget that she is someone today."
—Stacia Taucher

October 25, 2014

Your mom made me leave today. I've come to the point of driving her crazy, I think, so she made me get out of here for a while. I went to the mall and got her some new lotions from Bath and Body Works (brownie points, and ironically one was brownie scented). I stopped by Target to buy a pumpkin to decorate, since I now have a reputation to uphold in crafts. I decided on a fake one, so that it wouldn't rot, and we could keep it and set it out every year. Hopefully, we still have it! We (and by "we"

I of course mean "I") decorated the pumpkin with your name and some designs. It's received a lot of compliments already, and I pretend that it was no big deal (it was awesome).

At around 4, Papaw called to say they were going to drive up and bring us dinner. Apparently, your Mema is having a hard time staying away! They brought us Cracker Barrel and we sat in the cafeteria to eat.

I'm beginning to get nervous about the whole "baby-raising" thing that apparently is required of parents. Being totally honest, I know more about proton fusion than I do about miniature humans. If you told me that babies actually come from another solar system to steal all our pots and pans, I'd distract you with a smoke bomb long enough to go hide our new Rachel Ray set.

I began my formal training the day I found out you were coming. I bought several books in an attempt to broaden the miniscule knowledge I possess on the subject. The one thing I've taken from them is that all the horrors I could possibly imagine are many times normal for a baby. They're simply there to scare the crap out of you. You could stop breathing for several seconds at a time: normal. You will slam her head into multiple objects: this is expected. You could burst into flames at a moment's notice: perfectly fine.

To this point I've read a total of 5 books, and remain overwhelmingly lost. Not one chapter was dedicated to proper diaper changing. Not a single paragraph mentioned how to adequately apply a onesie. If by some miracle I manage to keep you alive, I plan on starting a "Novice Dad" boot camp- complete with obstacle courses, gas chambers, and rucksacks. I plan on hiring seasoned mothers as the drill sergeants, and can already hear their screams in my sleep- "COME ON MAGGOTS, GET THAT POOP CLEANED UP!! GO, GO, GO!! DROP DOWN AND GIVE THAT BABY 100 BELLY RASPBERRIES AND 25 BUTTERFLY KISSES, PRIVATE!!!"

GAVIN McDONALD

"A baby will make love stronger, days shorter, nights longer, bankroll smaller, home happier, clothes shabbier, the past forgotten, and the future worth living for."
—Anonymous

October 27, 2014

Well, here we are two weeks in, and the doctors told us this morning that we're staying for at least one more week to make it until 35 weeks. I hope I make it that long before your mom ends up stabbing me with her crossword pencil. Last night we got the awful news that Oscar Taveras, a Cardinals outfielder, was killed in a car accident. This was his first year as a Cardinal, but he was a player that baseball had ranked the top prospect in all of baseball. The Cardinals organization said he would be the next Albert Pujols. He was only 22 years old. So, that really sucks and I was depressed most of the day, which your mommy would never understand.

I went down to Busch Stadium to pay my respects. Hundreds of people had placed flowers, cards, jerseys, candles, and pictures at the Musial statue.

It's Halloween this Friday! Halloween has always been one of my favorite holidays. It would actually be pretty sweet if you were born on that day. My own little goblin (just a play on words, I hope you don't actually turn out resembling a goblin). I told your mom that I would like to paint her belly on Friday, and go around to the other rooms Trick-or-Treating… she said she would think about it. (You'll find out that this means 'no').

I'm worried it's going to be another very long week. I really need to go back to work, but I know as soon as I do, mommy will go into labor and by the time I show up I'll have missed the birth, your first words, and possibly your wedding day (it's a long drive) - and no one else is cutting that cord besides ME! I'll do my best not to give you an outie bellybutton. Those are gross. By some chance you DO end up with an outie, then I'll have to probably come back and edit this part out.

> *"Making the decision to have a child, it's momentous. It is to decide forever to have your heart go walking around outside your body."*
> —Elizabeth Stone

October 29, 2014

Your mom had a pretty rough day today. She's felt crummy with on and off contractions, pain in her hips, and constant nausea. They've checked her a couple times, but remains at 3 cm dilation. She made me leave for a while, because I was apparently driving her crazy, again. "Okay, I love you, but you need to leave, now." I decided to get my haircut, and then went to GameStop to get a few new Xbox games. I'm tired of reading and playing games on my phone! I have to charge the dang thing about 3 times in the course of one afternoon, and the heat emanating from it could very possibly fry an egg. If we happen to be here for a couple more weeks, I'm going to need some different types of entertainment, and I can't juggle. Not yet. Crap, now I have to go back to the mall for some juggling balls.

Mommy's friends Emily and Melissa came tonight to visit and brought us some dinner. The Royals were able to take the World Series to a deciding game 7, but were unable to seal the deal, and lost to the stupid Giants. The best part of the night was the Krispy Kreme donuts they brought us as well, except that I've made my keyboard extremely stickkkyyy.

"There are two things we should give your children; one is roots, and the other is wings."
—Hodding Carter

PART 2

The Arrival

October 30, 2014

11:45 Well, well, well....TODAY IS THE DAY WE'VE BEEN WAITING FOR!!! For the first time in 3 weeks, we actually got to sleep in for a while this morning. I got up and took a shower, and got all our clothes together to go to the death trap - err, laundromat. Your mom was feeling good with no complaints for the first time in weeks. I got to the first floor of the hospital, she called me and said, "Um, I need you to come back up here and look at this." When I got back to the room, she was sitting in the bathroom with soaked pants. The water has finally broken!

I'm sure your mom will remind everyone that I didn't believe her for quite a while, thinking she accidentally peed on herself. That's when she showed me the tiny, dark, curly hairs that ware in the water. I was half ecstatic knowing this was it, but also half nervous that we were in fact having a poodle. At that point, it seemed like everything went into overdrive. They moved us immediately to a new room in Labor and Delivery. I had about 47 loads of crap to move, and by the time I got to the new room, I was soaked in sweat, and had to change shirts.

I had already told the family that at the given time, they would receive a text message from me to let them know to get on the road. I've been waiting 3 weeks to send it and finally got my chance this morning.

THE ARRIVAL

I sent, "CODE KINLEY, THIS IS NOT A DRILL!!" We got to the new room, where they started the IV and began antibiotics.

12:30 I was suddenly transformed into an early century telephone operator, switching between calls left and right. Your Papa Jordan is on his way. I called your Mema and Papaw McDonald and they said they were also running towards the car! Your Aunt Christy said they would be leaving Salem as soon as school was out. They plan on starting the Pitocin at around 4:00 this afternoon. I keep saying that I really want you to be a Halloween baby, but your mom does NOT.

2:00 Mema, Papaw and Papa just showed up. Mema can't stop touching your mommy's belly, rubbing it down like prepping a Thanksgiving turkey. She is more than excited! They began mommy on the medicine to induce labor, and the contractions are now about 5 minutes apart. I walked down to craft class to let our friends know that we were close to having a baby, so they could forget about the bows today.

Your mom is beginning to hurt a little bit, but is trying to hold off getting the epidural as long as she can. She's a trooper, that's for sure. It's all just a waiting game now. We're just sitting here in the room, staring at each other. I keep joking that Papaw and I are going to run to the mall and then out to eat, and to call us if anything changes. Your mom isn't thinking we're too funny, so I've decided to water down my antics for a little while. She's taking this extremely serious for some reason.

4:45 Contractions are now 3 minutes apart and dilated to a 4. I ran down to the gift shop and bought some "It's A Girl" gum cigars for your arrival. Aunt Christy and her whole clan are on their way up now. We put a status on Facebook a couple hours ago, and everyone is going nuts (I half expected Mark Zuckerburg to send me a Cease and Desist letter, saying we're close to crashing the site). Needless to say, with all the difficulties we've had, you're already quite the celebrity back home. The last time they checked your mom, the doctor said, "Wow, she's definitely got a ton of hair!" Your Papa Jordan said he might have to go to the store and buy some Nair.

6:00 The epidural was just placed and Mommy's starting to feel slightly better. The contractions are now 1-2 minutes apart, and dilated to a 5. I'm sitting here watching Halloween on AMC Fear Fest, but your mom made me turn it on mute.

7:00 Well, the epidural didn't take. Mommy started having severe pain with the contractions. The anesthesiologist came and placed a second epidural, and so far is doing much better. I'm feeding her ice chips and massaging her feet! Yep, I'm pretty awesome.

10:00 Your mom is doing great, but remains at 5 cm dilation. You have definitely not made one thing easy so far, so why should you start now?! Remind me to spank you later. Aunt Christy and her whole fam showed up around 7:30. She can NOT wait to get her hands on you! Your Mema is also having a really tough time staying out of the room. She is fit to be tied. Between them two, we very well might have to set up one of those "Take a Number" stands, like at the DMV, for after you're born. We were all famished, so we got Pizza Hut delivered, and ate out in the waiting room, so we wouldn't be eating in front of your also starving mother. It's looking more and more like you will be a Halloween baby! My sweet little goblin (again no indication of possible appearance intended).

10:30 Big change, you might be coming quicker than we thought. Just did a check and she's now at a 9! Somewhere I heard the song began to play in my head from the movie Newsies, "Open the gates and seize the day!" I keep telling her to hold off as long as possible for midnight, and she keeps telling me to shut up about it, but you may very well have different plans. I love you so much already, my sweet princess. I will see you soon.

12:45 Your mom has been trying to push you out since 11:15. We really thought you were going to trick us all and come quick (Haha, "trick" us all...Halloween... get it?), but we've figured out a long time ago that you're not going to do ANYTHING easy! You are definitely now going to be a Halloween baby though! (Mommy's not too happy

THE ARRIVAL

about that, but I am elated.) She is resting now, and we'll begin to push again in about 15 minutes. Your cousins Natalie, Noah, and Neely are all sleeping in the waiting room, and the others are just sitting there waiting. In the pushes, I have noticed your dark hair though. Ugh, I am over ready for you to be here. Come quickly sweets!

> *"Certain is it that there is no kind of affection so purely angelic as of a father to a daughter. In love to our wives there is desire; to our sons, ambition, but to our daughters there is something which there are no words to express."*
> —Joseph Addison

October 31, 2014

My sweet little pumkin. At 1:00 in the morning, they made your mom take a break from pushing, as she was really starting to wear out. The nurse, Jaime, decided to try a different method where she and mommy would pull against each other using a sheet like "Tug-Of-War" style. I have to admit, I was doing everything I could to not laugh, with you too looking like ancient aborigines, grunting and yelling while trying to steal the others fabric. At 2:03 in the morning, you finally made your much awaited worldwide debut! As soon as you came out, you started SCREAMING your lungs out. I got to cut your cord, which proved to be much tougher than I thought. Your mother just managed to push a human out of her special place and here's sissy dad struggling to cut a small piece of skin with surgical scissors.

They began cleaning you off (which proved much rougher than I had expected: they looked like they were drying off a dog after its bath) and you topped the scale at 6 pounds and 3 ounces, much more than we had expected. They had to do some stitching on your mom (nope, no need for details or specifics here, so just keep right on reading), so she was able to finally hold you after about 30 minutes. I know I may be a bit biased, but man oh man, are you gorgeous.

They had to take you to the NICU for admission, so we were finally able to come visit you at 4:00, along with your grandparents and Aunt Christy and cousins shortly after that. They are very strict on the rules, so we have to scrub our arms and hands for two minutes up to the elbows before we can see you. I was pretending to be a surgeon getting ready to save a life, and kept yelling "SCALPEL", but again mommy wasn't ready for the wise cracks, so I need to hold off a little longer. We have to also take off all our rings and watches, and wear a hospital gown to hold you. I can't describe how tired we both were when we finally made it back to our room at around 8:00. We were able to take a short 1 hour nap, before we were up again and itching to get back to you.

The rest of the day consisted mainly on trying to get you to breast feed. The staff in the NICU kept calling you the "Rockstar" of the group, since you were over twice the size of all the other babies there. It's so hard to not just sit there and stare at you for hours, which is exactly what we do.

I had the opportunity to have you all to myself for a couple hours, while your mom went back to the room to rest a while. I sat and talked to you non-stop. We talked about the Cardinals, and how I expect you to be a die-hard fan. I explained to you how much God had blessed us with you, and that he protected you and mommy from everything that could have gone wrong. I told you that you need to spend your life thanking him. I also cried. I cried a lot.

My whole life has always been about me. I'll be the first to tell anyone that I've always had this problem of being selfish and wanting

THE ARRIVAL

it all. I bought whatever I wanted, I went wherever I wanted, and did whatever I wanted. For the first time, I didn't care. It was as if God flipped a switch in my life, and turned me upside down. I'll never be the same. I love your mom with everything that I have, but I didn't love her immediately. After months of dating, I realized I loved her and wanted to spend the rest of my life with her. But you... I loved you instantly. I became madly and deeply in love instantly.

My heart hurt when I was with you with love, and hurt when I was away from you with longing to have you again. The time I was able to spend with you was never enough, and the time I had to be away from you was always too much. For the first time, I couldn't care less about myself. I couldn't care less about the next car that I buy, the next job that I have, the next house I may live in. I couldn't care less if I make a million dollars or a hundred, if I'm famous or a nobody. You instantaneously became everything. Within seconds, my whole world was stuffed into a 6 pound baby. I'll never be the same. I love you, my little punkin. Happy birthday.

"Through the blur, I wondered if I was alone or if other parents felt the same way I did - that everything involving our children was painful in some way. The emotions, whether they were joy, sorrow, love or pride, were so deep and sharp that in the end they left you raw, exposed and yes, in pain. The human heart was not designed to beat outside the human body and yet, each child represented just that - a parent's heart bared, beating forever outside its chest."
—Debra Ginsberg

November 1, 2014

You had a very busy day today! If there had been a Party City close, I probably would have called to see if they carried "1 Day Birthday" supplies. We go down to feed you every three hours, and then your mom has to come back to pump right after. You've lost a little weight, so you're now just less than 6 pounds. They have to make sure that you can maintain your weight, eat properly, and maintain an adequate temperature before they can send you home. We put you in a new outfit today, but you threw up on it within about 3 seconds, so we quickly put you back into the supplied hospital gown.

You had a lot of visitors today that were anxious to hold and love on you. Papa Jordan, Mema and Papaw McDonald (not a shocker), Aunt Christy (again, not a shocker), and Emily all got their chance to finally get their hands on you (after following mommy's scrupulous hand sanitizing measures). Mema simply held you and cried. Papaw held you and laughed. Papa J held you for about 13 seconds because he was a little nervous. Aunt Christy held you while doing a full-blown photo shoot. It's the age of Facebook, so all pictures are immediately updated to the page to share with everyone. I wonder what social network will be popular when you grow up? Your original picture that I put on my wall for your announcement of birth got over 600 "likes". Yep, you're pretty much already famous, as "likes" equal popularity, obviously.

> *"One hundred years from now, it will not matter what my bank account was, the sort of house I lived in, or the kind of car I drove. But the world may be different because I was important in the life of a child."*
> —Forest E. Witcraft

PART 3

GOING HOME

November 3, 2014

Three days. You came home after a mere three days in the NICU. If I've said it once, I've said it a thousand times in the last couple months: "Seriously? Wow, that's awesome!" You were slightly jaundiced yesterday and today, but after 24 hours of light therapy (baby tanner) your bilirubin levels are low enough to go home. It took me around 26 hours to pack up all the junk we had accumulated over the last month of living in the hospital, and began our discharge teaching. We finally left the hospital around 5 in the evening.

The ride home was a weird one. I kept forgetting that you were back there. It was surreal. I kept remembering I had a "Baby on Board" and instantly wanted to run into the nearest Walmart and grab the window decal that stated the same. We swung through McDonald's to grab a bite and headed for Rolla. I'm surprised you couldn't talk by the time you got home though as slow as I was driving. I half expected to open the back door and you hit me with, "Geez dad! We were passed by an Amish carriage filled with nuns!"

I walked in the door with you, and it hit me. You were mine. I got to keep you! I was afraid that at the last minute, the doctors would come around and say something like, "Mr. McDonald, I'm sorry, but the board has determined that your level of maturity and baby knowledge is far too low to allow you any attempt in raising another human being." I walked you around the house for your grand tour. It was strange, like I was entertaining a very tiny house guest that kept farting, and pretending she didn't hear it.

Neither I nor your mom slept much that night, of course. We just laid there and stared at you. Every now and then I would kind of poke your side to make sure you were breathing (don't tell mom). I might have to go the Apple store tomorrow and upgrade to the new iPhone with 5,000G of storage for the ridiculous amount of pictures I'm going to take.

We are never ceased to be amazed at God's unending favor and faithfulness to us. You were premature. You were supposed to have complications and a lengthy hospital stay. You were supposed to be underweight and malnourished. It's at this time that I'm reminded of how astonishing our God is. Pumkin, you must never forget that. He is the one that looks at the situation, the trial or tribulation that we are standing in, and simply grins. He loves to take the "This is what's *supposed* to happen…" and do the opposite.

The headline of our story was supposed to be disastrous, not magical. The story was intended to be terrible, but ended up being tremendous. God is the one that shows up during our worst circumstances, and reminds us that the story we heard from the enemy is not the story that we have to live out. He stands there in is immeasurable power and love and declares that HE is the publisher, the editor, the photographer of our story, and HE is the creator of our chapters. When you find yourself staring at inevitable trouble, simply read that first line on the first page of your story. It is being written by your father, and he is one amazing author. You must never forget that.

> *"You may speak but a word to a child, and in that child there may be slumbering a noble heart which shall stir the Christian Church in years to come."*
> —Charles Spurgeon

November 7, 2014

It's been a crazy few days. Okay, that's a lie. We've actually just done that same few things over and over again for the last 72 hours. We feed you, we try to sleep at least 2 straight hours at various times during the day or night, and we change your diaper. That's pretty much it. But the crazy thing is, is that I am loving every second of it. Don't worry; I know there will come a day of "Awe, geez Kin! Again?! I changed you 9 seconds ago!"

Your poor mother is having a little difficulty in trying to breast feed you. Don't tell her I told you this, but even though her boobs are ginormous right now, the actual "milk dispenser mechanisms" are too small, so she has to wear this weird plastic shell thing so that you get a good latch! She's constantly ticked off about it, because it keeps falling off causing your breakfast to leak down her stomach. I try to act supportive, I really do…but I'm earnestly just sitting across the room, and laughing hysterically on the inside.

November 15, 2014

It's been a productive week. And by productive, I of course mean we've simply sat around and stared at you - especially your mom. She literally can't take her eyes off of you. You know why? Because you're perfect. The jury is still out on who you look like. There are some that say you're my spitting image. Your Grandma Jordan (can't remember what she wants to be called) has actually been calling you "Gavin," thinking you favor your good ole Dad. Then others say you're a mirror image of your mom. Want to know my honest opinion? I have no clue. I think you look like a baby (thank God that whole "Goblin" thing didn't happen).

You continue to projectile vomit with every single feeding. It's become a common place for us. This is gross, but also kind of funny: Whenever you burp, Evie, our miniature wiener dog, comes running from whatever blanket she happens to be sleeping under and licks up your puke. I have a literal Pavlov's dog on my hands – I am expecting her to start salivating with any future bodily function noise from you. Stinking nasty. I keep getting on to your mom for letting her do it, but truthfully, I do it too. It's just much easier, and Evie seems to really enjoy it. If I happen to start using the breast milk in my oatmeal, Mommy would literally be feeding the whole family.

It was a big day for you, because you got your newborn pictures taken. It was at some girl's house that your mom knows, and she actually did a really good job. The only problem we had is that you wouldn't keep your daggum tongue in your mouth. It reminded me of a snake aimlessly licking the air around him to get a sense of his surroundings. I could imagine you thinking, "Hmmm… (lick, lick)…I haven't thrown up here… (lick, lick)…Or farted here… (lick, lick)" Don't know what your deal is with your ADHD tongue, but it easily turned a 1 hour photo session into 3. And yes, a lot of them were naked pics, so I apologize in advance for showing them off to any stupid boy you may bring home.

November 19, 2014

Today was a very bitter sweet day for me. The day I went back to work. (Dum, Dum, DUUUUUM!!) I missed my job terribly (never thought I actually would), but I was starting to go into withdraws for blood, codes, guts, and adrenaline. It was an extremely long day, and couldn't wait to get back home to you, but you've definitely given me reason to work that much harder. To show you what it means to have an excellent work ethic, to give everything you've got, and always remember why you do it.

I was reminded today of why I became a nurse. I had a newborn baby, not much older than you that coded in my ER. I saved that little girl today. That's why, as much as it hurts when I leave you for work in the morning, I continue to do what I do. I literally save lives, and could never be more proud of the choices that I've made to lead me to this point in my life.

Sweets, I've made some stupid mistakes, and someday when you're older I will tell them to you. But those mistakes are what molded me into what I am now. Trust me, I'm far from perfect. I have a short temper at times, I'm selfish, I haven't been going to church like I should, and so on. But you've given me a reason to try harder. To try harder with everything. To love your mom more, to pray more often, to be healthier, to give more time, to speak kinder to people, to quit judging so quickly. You may very well become my saving grace. Thank you, Punkin.

> *"I believe that what we become depends on what our fathers teach us at odd moments, when they aren't trying to teach us. We are formed by little scraps of wisdom."*
> —Umberto Eco

PART 4

THE HOLIDAYS

November 27, 2014

It's your first Turkey Day! I wanted to trace your hand with a crayon, so you could make a turkey out of it, but with them still being so small, it would just end up looking like a canary. I can't wait for the years when you will actually enjoy and appreciate all the crazy traditions that have been passed down from my parents. You're not even a month old yet, but I insisted on propping you up in front of the TV so you could watch the Macy's Thanksgiving Day Parade, and then jumping up and down with you when the "real" Santa come up at the end. Needless to say, you were not interested. You only cared about how much vomit you could possibly soak into the new clothes that were just put on you.

    Your mom was still not keen on the idea of taking you out of the house (between you and me, she went a little crazy about keeping you away from all human contact for a while.) After a couple heated exchanges, and yes mommy's and daddy's have them from time to time, she agreed to go to Mema and Papaw's house for lunch. If they made portable bubbles for babies, like the kinds for people with terminal diseases, I'm sure she would have ordered you one. I was really hoping she would come around to agreeing since your Uncle Nathan, Aunt Amy, and cousins Jake, Ayla, and Easton have yet to meet you. It's their year to be here, so I'm looking forward to finally getting to show you off a little bit.

THE HOLIDAYS

Amy couldn't let you go. She was in love at first sight, but that's easy for her. She, like your own Mommy, was born to be a parent. Uncle Nathan was even pretty happy to hold you, and kept saying how pretty you were. Your cousin Ayla was also quite taken. She got to hold you for a while, and soaked up every second. Uncle Nathan called me later and said that she was running around with her doll, calling it Kinley, and shouting, "I've got to find the gas drops!" I wish I would have thought to buy stock in gas drops before you were born, because we go through quite a large amount of it.

Papaw prayed his usual prayer that made us all cry before we ate, and then all settled in for an amazing dinner that Papaw managed all on his own. He's still trying to figure out all the ins and outs of cooking, but he's actually doing a really good job. Mema is right by him constantly trying to correct him, though! Of course, as SOON as we began eating, you started to cry. I held you for the rest of the meal, and honestly couldn't have been happier to do so, although I did accidentally drop a green bean on your head at one point. I didn't tell Mom…

> *"What it's like to be a parent: It's one of the hardest things you'll ever do, but in exchange it teaches you the meaning of unconditional love."*
> —Nicholas Sparks

December 5, 2014

Well, today was a first. Your mom and I decided to go on a much needed date. We settled on Love Sushi in Jefferson City, and your Aunt Teetee came over to babysit! (She's going by Aunt Teetee now, because it's too hard to say Christy. It's cute, but all I think when I hear it is boobs.) She was SO excited to spend some time with you. She came in with snacks, a book, and ready to love on you as much as she could. She'd packed enough that we could have gone to actual *China* for sushi. I begged her to let me pay her, but she wasn't having it. She insisted that this was a vacation for her to get away from the constant madness that is the Leathers Clan!

After your mommy kissed your face about a zillion times, we left. We made it to KOI Sushi here in Rolla, and decided to just eat there instead. We were back home within an hour! Baby steps for your mom are needed, I've found. Your Aunt Teetee was definitely not expecting us so soon, elbow deep in orange Cheeto dust and engrossed in a Lifetime movie.

I really don't know what we're going to do when we have to take the Christmas lights down. You can stare at them for hours. I'm going to end up being one of those losers that has their lights up until Easter. You've already got a couple presents under the tree! We've decided to not spend too much on you this year, since you really have no idea what's going on, so we're spending money on each other. I gave your mom a list of everything I want, but keep adding to it. There's so much cool stuff out there, and I'm just a 10 year old boy stuck in this aging old man. If my wife wouldn't make so much fun of me, I'd love to have that new K'nex connector set or Lego Batman for the Xbox.

"Perhaps it takes courage to raise children..."
—John Steinbeck

THE HOLIDAYS

December 19, 2014

Only 5 more sleeps until Christmas! I know you're excited, you just don't know how to show it yet. We tried our best to hit some traditions this year, but with you still being so small, we were limited on how much we could actually do. We really wanted to get your picture taken with Santa, but with the Flu virus at all-time record numbers this year, we opted out of succumbing you to the illness. But we were able to watch about all the necessary movies. We attempted to again prop you up in front of the television, but you were too busy farting to be able to hear anything that was going on. (It's got to be the abnormal amount of gas drops.)

We did, however, fit in Christmas cookie decorating, though. We went to Mema and Papaw's tonight for the annual ritual of decorating the candy cane, Santa, stocking, and Christmas tree shaped sugar cookies (and the occasional one that comes out with the unknown shape that we end up decorating as a pile of poop after mixing all the colors at the end). I can't wait to show you my world-renowned skills, and pass on the amazing talent to you. Papaw enjoyed holding you the entire time, and you shockingly stayed awake for the entirety of the event. Neely even made one in your honor by getting as many sprinkles as possible on a single cookie.

Aunt Teetee made her typical perfect, one color, one type of sprinkle, boring cookies. I made my typical award-winning, "Food Network" worthy cookies. Noah made a Cardinals cookie, which almost made me tear up at how proud of him I was. Your mother, of course, chose not to participate. She's been around the family for about 3 years now, but still has yet to come completely out of her shell!

GAVIN McDONALD

"To be in your children's memories tomorrow, you have to be in their lives today."
—Barbara Johnson

December 25, 2014

It's your first of MANY amazing Christmas's. Santa definitely came, and we were up (much to the chagrin of your Mommy) bright and early at 6 am. We opened our gifts to each other first, and decided to open yours later when we get home from the Grandparents so your Nonni (which I finally found out is what your Grandma Jordan wants to be called- Italian for Grandma) could see you open them.

I got a new Espresso Coffee machine, as if I could possibly need any more caffeine! I also got a new shaving kit, since I'm hairy beyond what's normal for any human being. I really hope I don't pass this curse on to you. Sadly, it very well may happen, given the amount of dark hair on your back above your butt crack. I asked your mom if I could shave it off before you got your newborn pictures, but she of course, said absolutely not. Maybe I'll just do it one day when she's at work- she'll never know.

I also got a new wedding band that looks like a baseball with stitches! I was blown away! It's the exact ring that I had always wanted before we got married, but since we ran away to Gatlinburg, we had to get rings quickly from JC Penny's, so I settled on another type. Your mom actually went all "Shawshank Redemption" on me and cut out the middle of a book and placed the ring inside! Needless to say, I was extremely impressed.

I got your mom a North Face jacket, at a whopping $250!! Seriously?! A jacket that's $250? That's ridiculous, but it's what she wanted, so she got it. I also got her some new tennis shoes, a pan, a ring holder, and some other junk. I was so excited for her to open the jacket, because I had her convinced that I didn't get it. She was pumped when she opened it, but it was way too small, and yes we're blaming you.

We got to Mema and Papaw's by eight o'clock. Papaw had scalded the green beans, so the whole house smelled pretty bad. Poor guy is not having very good luck. You got a hedgehog toy, an elephant walker thing, and a Raggedy Ann doll. Needless to say, you got passed around a lot today. The Christmas bow on your head was so large that it covered the vast majority of your face. From your mommy and daddy you also got a play mat that you lay on, a bouncing thingy that you'll eventually be able to ride, and a pink piggy bank. I'm excited for when you actually will enjoy toys, because right now it's just another object for you to puke on. Merry Christmas, Punkin.

"Nothing I've ever done has given me more joys and rewards than being a father to my children."
—Bill Cosby

December 31, 2014

Your very first New Years. What a crazy year it has been, and definitely one that I will never forget, that's for sure. It's felt like I've been on a rollercoaster ride for 12 months. There were times that I wasn't sure if I was going to make it, and I don't say that lightly. I remember times of sitting in the bathroom and crying for what seemed like hours.

I would sit and think about mom, and how much I miss her, though she's still here…kind of. I would think about what it would be like if she had never had the stroke, and would be able to watch you, feed you, hold you, and take you on vacations. I would think about Dad, and how much he's changed this year. The smile I've seen on his face lately is one that has been placed on intentionally when we're around, not one that is naturally there because he's happy. I would think about your mom, and wonder if she still loved me as much as she used to, and pray that she would also find that missing part of her heart that seemed to also steal her smile somewhere along the way. I would think about you and wonder if everything would be okay. Wonder if you would come out healthy and strong. Wonder what would happen to my life if, by chance, you didn't make it. I think about God, and how much I miss him, church, worship, fellowship, and everything that goes with it.

I've become so complacent, and I always promised myself I wouldn't let that happen, yet here I am. I promise to raise you in a Godly home, but there definitely needs to be a change within me, before I can lead you to him. I must change my own heart, so that you will be able to see how I love and serve him in my daily life, and hopefully you'll follow my example. 2014 was an amazing year. It gave me the greatest gift I could have ever asked for in you- although this new ring is pretty sweet too.

> *"Train up a child in the way he should go;
> even when he is old he will not depart from it"*
> —Proverbs 22:6

PART 5

A Brand New Year

January 8, 2015

Well, I had to call the aborigine's in Africa to apologize for the crying I'm sure they heard from you today. Two month old shots! To be honest, I was more worried about your mother today. I figured I'd have to have her placed in a straight jacket and committed to the psych ward, but she actually did surprisingly well. You're finally in the double digits for weight, tipping the scales at a whopping 10 pounds today, and I'm going to guess about 7 of those pounds is in your double chin- you can thank your Dad for that trait.

One trait you *didn't* get from your dear old Dad is the fact that you poop approximately once a week. That's crazy. I have no idea how you could continue to eat! I keep waiting for the day that your spit up is brown. I know it's coming. We asked Dr. No-Smile if this was okay, and he didn't seem concerned, so I guess we'll just keep waiting.

> *"You can learn many things from children.*
> *How much patience you have, for instance."*
> —Franklin P. Jones

January 12, 2015

POOP WATCH 2015!! The topic of our daily discussion and thoughts is none other than you pooping- or you NOT pooping actually (oh, how far we've come). You have been incredibly fussy the last couple days, and we are sure this is the reason. We are currently on day 5 of no action, and we're checking diapers every time you fart- which happens to be approximately every 14 seconds.

We've taken to asking friends and family for some home remedy solutions, so we've now tried everything: massaging the belly, taking your rectal temperature, Pedialyte, pushing legs up into your stomach, peppermint water, Karo syrup, and (sorry about this) stimulating your little bottom hole with lubricant. Still nothing. The only thing it's managed to do is tick you off.

"Parents need to fill a child's bucket of self-esteem so high that the rest of the world can't poke enough holes to drain it dry."
—Alvin Price

January 13, 2015

It's the day that your mother has been dreading since the day you were born- the day she goes back to work. And it also happens to be the day I'VE been dreading as well- the day I'm alone with you for 13 hours. It's all up to dad, and that scares the POOP out of me (wish it did you). What's crazy is that I am responsible for people's lives on a daily basis. I deal with traumatic injuries, dying people, choking infants, blood and guts without batting an eye. But this has got me frazzled. I think it's because no matter how crazy things get in the ER, I always feel some control over what's going on. When you start crying and I don't know how to help you, I feel worthless and out of control. Hopefully you'll give me an easy first day.

"Raising children is an uncertain thing; success is reached only after a life of battle and worry."
—Democritus

January 14, 2015

What an adventurous day, Punkin! It's day two of daddy/daughter day, and it's been interesting to say the least. As I'm sure you know now, I have a little touch of ADHD (and by little touch, I mean I was dipped into the concentrated version at birth). I absolutely love to spend the entire day with you, but being stuck in this house for 13 hours is going to be really hard for me to not go entirely insane. I'm not to the point yet of feeling comfortable enough to go anywhere alone with you, so I'm a prison in my own home.

For some reason, you hate to be laid down (sure it has something to do with never leaving the confines of your mom and Nonni's arms), but I had a lot of stuff I needed to get done around the house. So, I decided to attempt the weird baby wrap thing that my cousin Drake got us (it's Cardinals, of course). I had to watch the YouTube tutorial a few dozen times before I got it right, but then it was AWESOME! You weren't sure about it at first, but you quickly went to sleep, and I was ecstatic. I got all the laundry done, cleaned and picked up the house, read some of my

A BRAND NEW YEAR

latest parenting book, and even got a couple Xbox hours in. Although, I'm pretty sure it was way too tight, so I had to continuously check your feet for adequate circulation.

At about 6:00, I was getting stuff ready to make dinner, and your mom called and said your Papa had been in a bad car accident, and didn't know how bad he was. I called up to the ER to see if they'd heard anything yet. They said they were flying two from the scene, knew Paul was involved, but didn't know if he was one of the critical patients yet. I remember kneeling in your room while you were sleeping, and praying for your Papa. I've never seen him as excited about anything as he is about you. He absolutely adores his grandbaby. I began picturing the possibility of you never getting the chance to actually know him, and it broke my heart.

About an hour later, a nurse from the ER called and let me know that he was not one of the patients that had to be flown, and was on his way by ambulance into the ER in Rolla. That heavy weight and lump in my throat finally began to fade. He was going to be okay, just really banged up. Then I heard about one of the passengers in another car that was 8 months pregnant. The crash killed the baby boy inside of her. Before a few months ago, I would have thought it was sad. But now having you here, the thought of losing you so young made me absolutely sick. I can't imagine what that mom is going through, and my heart literally hurt for her. Today could have ended very different. Our whole lives could have been changed instantly, but God definitely had his hand on your Papa today, which gives us yet one more reason to love and thank him with our lives. God is good all the time, and all the time, God is good.

"Each day of our lives we make deposits in the memory banks of our children".
—Charles Swindoll

January 15, 2015

Today will be a day that will live in infamy forever. If I told anyone besides your mother what a big deal this was to us, they would never fully understand. You pooped. Wait, you didn't just poop, you exploded. I'm sure that from space a small breast milk mushroom cloud could be seen from the satellites above Rolla, Missouri.

Today was day 8, and we had had enough. You were completely miserable, constantly crying, and couldn't sit still. It felt like there was a baseball in your poor little belly, it was so distended. We decided to go against the pediatrician's suggestion, and try a liquid suppository. We were nervous, because the box said to consult your doctor before administering to babies under 2 years old… you are about 21 months too young, but we were desperate ("It's okay everyone, I'm a nurse!").

We got all set up on the changing pad in your room, and decided to only give you half the dose, since you were so young. I thought about placing a paint drop cloth on the floor, and plastic up on the walls, preparing for the occasion like Dexter does before cuts up a victim on his show, but I ran out of time. Yes, I'm aware that I tend to exaggerate slightly on occasion, but this is the God-honest truth: it took 20 seconds. You went full-blown "Old Faithful" and began to squirt like your life depended upon it. I had visions of a rookie firefighter that let the water hose accidentally get away from him, and it was flying around uncontrollably. If I had known it was going to be such an impressive occurrence, I would have sold tickets and set up some bleachers in your room ("Popcorn! Cotton Candy! Poncho! Umbrella!"). You were filling up diapers faster than I could get new ones under you. After topping off about 8 diapers (no joke here surprisingly), you were finally done. Your belly looked all sunk in, like you hadn't ate for weeks. It was instant relief for you. You were able to relax, and so could we. I'm trying to decide whether to call it POOPACALYPSE or POOPAGEDDEN, because this day definitely needs a name and to be remembered for years to come. Still upset I didn't sell tickets, because now we have to go get a new box of diapers.

> *"Trust yourself. You know more than you think you do."*
> —Benjamin Spock

January 20, 2015

Another day with Dad! Mom left for work at 6 in the morning, and you began to cry at about 6:04. I had heard a trick once to use shirts that the mom had worn to try to soothe a crying baby. It was worth a shot! I grabbed an old shirt of mommy's out of the laundry basket and draped it on my chest. You were crying hysterically, and then took a huge whiff of the shirt. It was like cotton magic. You stopped! You instantly became stoic and calm, and I was blown away. (Probably had something to do with the dried milk on the front). I took a picture and sent it to mommy, knowing it would make her day. I know you don't realize it, but you miss your mom terribly when she's gone. I know that you'll be madly in love with daddy someday, but for now- "mom's da bomb diggity", as she likes to say.

After that feat of pure genius on daddy's part, we had a great day. You can now look right into my eyes, and I know you see me. I could sit on this couch for hours, and stare into your beautiful eyes. You are now smiling and laughing, which melts my heart every time. I have to talk in this weird high-pitched voice constantly (which for some reason always ends up in a headache and sore neck), but it's totally worth it. If I've said "Are you happy?" or "You're so pretty!" once, I've said it a bazillion times- which is weird, because I could just as easily say something like, "I need to poop!" in that high voice, and you would still smile. Well, that's actually not the best analogy, since you're probably thinking that same thing...

You were in such a good mood, that I finally got to dress you up in one of my Cardinal's jerseys and hat. You suffered through it just long enough for me to get a good picture, which is all that matters. I sent it to mommy, which didn't think it was near as funny or awesome as I did... shocker. Maybe this daddy-keeping-baby thing isn't going to be near as terrifying as I thought it would be.

> *"No one is ever quite ready; everyone is always caught off guard. Parenthood chooses you. And you open your eyes, look at what you've got, say "Oh, my gosh," and recognize that of all the balls there ever were, this is the one you should not drop. It's not a question of choice."*
> —Marisa de los Santos

January 25, 2015

It's National Opposite Day! I'm somewhat peeved that this hasn't been declared a national holiday yet. Arbor Day can be observed, but not a day full of laughter and happiness due to the craziness of doing everything opposite of what's socially acceptable?! So, in honor of this soon-to-be holiday, I thought I would give some fatherly advice:

A BRAND NEW YEAR

Make sure you spend every dime you earn as quickly as you get it. Bills are stupid. They won't shut off the electric for a *good* three months, so you have a nice cushion there! Go crazy!

If you happen to change clothes, throw those clothes sporadically and haphazardly around the bedroom, hallway, and bathroom. It gives the house a certain "flair" and splash of color. Whatever you do, don't put them in the hamper. That's lame. Don't be lame.

When I let you officially date boys in 6th grade, make sure the lucky guy is at least 4 years older, so that he has a driver's license. That way, I'll save a lot on gas. Also, make sure he's in a band and has a Mohawk with several piercings, because that just sounds awesome.

Whenever you go out, make sure you have enough make-up on that I can't even recognize your face. You're a McDonald, so I expect you to look like Ronald for all dates. And when you finally come back home the next morning, try not to wake me.

School is actually a huge waste of time. Here's a short list of people without high school diplomas: Robert De Niro, Jay-Z, Billy Joel, Simon Cowell, Johnny Depp, Katy Perry, Nicolas Cage, Tom Cruise, Marilyn Monroe, John Travolta, and Frank Sinatra. You know what all these people have in common? They're rich and famous and awesome and cool. If I were you, I'd move to Hollywood as *soon* as possible to pursue your acting career.

Apply for as many credit cards as you can while you're young, then max them all out on electronics and food. Trust me, after not paying on them for a couple years, they'll eventually charge off and stop calling you.

During dinner time, never take your eyes off your phone. That way I won't have to ask you about your boring day, and you won't be forced into talking to us.

Whenever your boyfriend sneaks over to the house in the middle of the night, do not, and I repeat, do NOT leave the doors unlocked. That scares me.

If the police happened to be called to the house during a party you're throwing while mom and dad are out of town, do NOT tell them who the owner of the house is. That way, they can't charge me with anything.

While trying to decide on a career, be sure to choose the highest paid and not just the one that's going to make you happy. Myth: money doesn't buy happiness. Truth: Money buys jet skis, and jet skis equal happiness.

There's no reason to ever be tired. If you're tired, you're not on your 'A' game, so load up on caffeine pills, energy drinks, and sweets. You can sleep when you're dead.

If you happen to be a baseball fan, definitely go for the Cubs, because they're the best team in all of sports with the greatest fans. Or better yet, since baseball is so painstakingly boring, choose another sport- like NASCAR! Now THAT'S an exciting sport.

Run with scissors, leave every single light on in the house, chew tobacco, curse like a sailor, drive like a maniac while texting, practice Scientology, own a cat, laugh at fat people, park in handicap spots, pirate movies at the theatre, watch nothing but MTV and Lifetime, dress like a hooker, play with fire, blow dry your hair in the bathtub, bite your nails, steal out of the offering plate, hitchhike, get a tramp stamp tattoo, pierce your tongue, eat McDonald's daily, swim right after you eat, find a boyfriend online, forget the seatbelt, rip tags of mattresses, litter constantly, don't return shopping carts, burp and fart in public, and buy underwear at yard sales.

Whew, that was easy to do… Happy Opposite's Day, Son!

"As soon as I saw you, I knew an adventure was going to happen."
—Winnie the Pooh

A BRAND NEW YEAR

January 28, 2015

I spoke too soon about keeping you being easy. Mommy went to work, and you shortly after began to cry. I fed you, made sure your diaper was clean, got you warm, but you didn't stop. I rocked you, walked with you, sang to you, and you only got louder. I tried the mommy shirt trick, I got my guitar out and played it, I turned on cartoons, you screamed harder. I gave you gas drops, gripe water, Pedialyte, Tylenol, nothing was working. I massaged your belly, patted your back, rubbed your head, it was now noon and no relief. I tried your Momarro swing, your play mat, your crib, our bed, the recliner, the couch, but nope.

I was all out of options. I didn't know what to do. I was crying. I was tense and stressed. I was at the end of my rope and frustrated. I felt completely out of control and out of ideas. Your eyes were swollen from crying, and my heart was broken in defeat. I felt like a failure. For the first time since you were born, I felt like an utter failure as a father, and it killed me. I walked outside on the back deck and screamed. I screamed harder than I ever have. I couldn't honestly tell you if I was screaming at God, at you, at myself, at the situation, I don't know, but I had to scream. I yelled, "What do you want from me!? What could possibly be wrong?! I've done it all! I've tried everything, but you WON'T SHUT UP!!"

Then I began to cry. It was a deep, deep cry from my soul that had probably been building up for a long time. I cried because of today, I cried because of mom, and because of dad. I cried because I hate living here. I cried because I'd let God down so much in my life. I cried because of all the things I could have done better. I cried because I was supposed to be this amazing minister, and I cried because it feels like I've let everyone down. I cried because I have no close friends, and I cried because I've lost so many amazing ones over the years. I was kneeling in the rain on the porch a broken man, and don't know how to fix it. I cried for a long time. Today was rough. Today was a rough, rough day.

GAVIN McDONALD

> *"Lately all my friends are worried that they are turning into their fathers. I'm worried I'm not."*
> —Dan Zevin

February 5, 2015

There will be days that you will inevitably face in your life where you question that you've made the right choices. Now, I'm not talking about your Mommy, because I've never once questioned whether that was the right decision – she's truly the best thing ever. I'm talking about your choice in career. I'm so excited to see what road you decide to travel. Will you be a natural in school, and go on to make enough money to put daddy in a beautiful retirement home in California? Or will you have to work your tail off in your studies, and still just slide by enough to land a reasonable blue-collar job and live paycheck to paycheck like the majority of us?

I have no clue whether you'll be a doctor, or a waitress. A lawyer or a teacher. An entrepreneur or a nurse. I wonder every day the choices that you will make, because no matter what I want or wish for you, the choice is ultimately yours. The only thing I pray for is that you find something that brings you true joy. Is a doctor better than a waitress? It is, only if it makes you happy. Should you be a teacher besides a lawyer? Absolutely, if you find out that teaching is what fills that passion. One of the greatest things about this life that we're are given, is that we truly do write our own story. I want nothing more than for your story to be one filled with fulfillment, excitement, and joy.

Today, I questioned whether I had made the right choice on becoming an Emergency Room nurse, and guess what: you will also one day question your own. I was one hour from going home and we got the call of an infant coming in that wasn't breathing. I didn't think anything of it. I've dealt with parents that thought their kid "wasn't breathing" a thousand times that ultimately ended up in nothing. But then the EMS crew came rushing in the back door holding a one month old baby, and as soon as I saw him I knew it was bad.

The baby was white as a sheet, laying limp in the paramedics arms. I got him on the table as quick as I could and then I saw his face. He was beautiful. He was perfect. But he wasn't breathing and had no pulse. For a couple seconds I froze. I didn't freeze because I didn't know what to do. I didn't freeze because he was an infant. I froze because for a couple seconds, all I could see was you. All I could see was all the possibilities this baby could grow into and accomplish over the course of his life, and it was all hanging in the balance of my knowledge and skills.

We worked for an hour; the dad and mom at the end of the bed watching my every move, praying we knew enough and did enough to save their baby. But we didn't. The doctor stopped and looked up to the mom; the babies' mommy that carried him for 9 horrible months and endured torturing labor to finally deliver a healthy baby. The baby I was now holding, tubes coming from mouth and nose, needles in his tiny arms and legs, lying literally lifeless. All the dreams the parents had for their baby was over. And I felt like it was my fault. All I could feel was overwhelming grief and blame. The once loud and bustling trauma room went eerily silent as the doctor declared the time of death, and the mom fell to her knees in crippling heartbreak.

I've always been the strong one in the ER. I was never the one to break, shed a tear, or get emotionally involved. I was there to do a job, and I did it well. But today, as I stared at the baby in my arms, I wanted to run away and never come back. I ran to a storage room, slid to the floor behind the crutches and gauze, and wept. This isn't what I had signed up for. I didn't get paid enough for this. For the rest of my life, his beautiful face will be forever etched into my brain. I will never forget him.

But...and here's the point of my story: Am I going to go into work tomorrow? Yes, I am. Is the sadness gone? No. Are the guilt, blame, and heartache resolved? Not for a while. But even as terrible as it was and how much it will affect me forever, I still know that I have a job that touches everyone in their most vulnerable time of need. I still know that the hundreds that I do save far outweigh the few that I can't. There are few places that I can go in town where someone isn't running up to me and enveloping me in a true loving hug, saying "You are the one that saved my grandpa" or, "I'll never forget the passion you showed my mom." The happiness that fills my heart and warms my skin when this happens can never be replaced with a job that pays more, one that gets to travel everywhere or one that overlooks the ocean.

I am not telling you to become a nurse. I'm not even telling you to make sure you're in a job that helps people. All that I'm saying is to be part of something that, even when you're facing the hardest days, the happiness you find within all the junk changes you. Make sure the joy always outweighs the sadness. If you are ever to find yourself in a place of constant bad: pack your stuff, don't look back, and move on to something else. You will always have the opportunities in life for a "do over." Take advantage of them, but never treat them as failures. A failure is when you stay in a place of sadness. Life is way too short, and sadness way too heavy a load to bear. So, write your story and make it a good one. I'll be the old guy in the nursing home reading it, smiling from ear to ear, overwhelmed with deep pride and relentless joy. (Even more so, if you become a nurse.)

"You have brains in your head. You have feet in your shoes. You can steer yourself any direction you choose. You're on your own. And you know what you know. And YOU are the one who'll decide where to go..."
—Dr. Seuss

February 10, 2015

I'm slowly getting better at taking you places by myself. Mommy's working, and I had some errands to run, so I decided to brave all the things that plague my mind, and venture out with you into the wild. We went to Lowe's to grab a couple things for the house, and then into Walgreens to quickly buy a couple things for you girls for Valentine's Day. The hardest part is getting that impossible car seat into my 2-door crapmobile. With all the finagling and knocking around trying to get you latched in, I probably should have ran you through the ER real quick for a concussion check-up.

We made it home without a hitch, and I took you into your room to change your diaper. But then something happened that scared me more than I had been in a long time. I was doing my normal baby talk to you ("You're so pretty!"), trying to illicit a smile, when I heard a man talking in my back bedroom. I froze. There was someone in the house. My gun was, of course, on the nightstand in the bedroom.

For a second, I thought I'd imagined it, so I went back to cooing you. Then I heard him again, and knew I wasn't dreaming. I yelled, "I have a gun and I swear, I will shoot you!!" But when I heard the intruder yell back the exact same thing, I realized my immeasurable ignorance: the baby monitor was on in the bedroom and I was hearing my own voice in delay. I instantly recalled Jim Carrey in the "Grinch Who Stole Christmas" yelling and arguing at his own echoing voice. I looked down to see you grinning from ear to ear. Somewhere deep in your subconscious, you were laughing at Daddy. I'm sure the first of many times you'll have the opportunity to make fun of my stupidity.

> *"I cannot think of any need in childhood as strong as the need for a father's protection."*
> —Sigmund Freud

February 14, 2015

Happy Valentine's Day, sweets! I had to work today, so we celebrated Valentines and Daddy's birthday yesterday. We went to Jefferson City and ate at Red Lobster (I pray my next baby comes out a cheddar biscuit), then did a little shopping. You did so well! Think we're finally getting to the point where we can take you out to more places without crippling fear of the unknown. Mommy dressed you up in your Valentines outfit today and sent me a picture at work, and it has to be one of my favorite pictures so far. I was showing you off to everyone all day, whether they wanted to see it or not.

Before you were born, I was always the guy that HATED having to look at pictures of peoples kids. I would have to smear on my perfect fake smile, and say the appropriate "Oh my goodness, she is so precious!" phrases, when in actuality I couldn't have cared less. It was bad enough to have to look at one picture, but most parents (especially first time parents) would start flipping through the hundreds of extremely-similar photos that they took at bath time the night before. It was torture to the point I may have yelled "UNCLE!!" once or twice. But oh, how the tides have turned! I literally held up the Wal-Mart check-out line this week showing your new pictures to the random cashier. I have effectively filled the "proud dad" shoes extremely well. If only they had a "Honk If You Are So Proud Of Your Kid That You Want To Make A Statue Of Them And Place It In Times Square" bumper sticker, I'd be set! But my bumper isn't big enough...

A BRAND NEW YEAR

Your mom got me a new Cardinals book and a stand for my razor for my cake day. She also got me a 'Fitbit' bracelet to track my fitness! I'm trying desperately to lose weight. I've gained 40 pounds in the last year! That's what getting married AND having a baby within a 12-month span does to someone's psyche. What's really not fair is that your Mom somehow lost her baby weight within 3 months by eating ice cream and potato chips. I'm having a hard time losing a pound eating dirt and water.

I was excited to get you something for Valentines. I will be able to get you the typical candy and stuffed animals later when you'll actually appreciate it, but this year I wanted to do something special that you'll cherish the rest of your life. I got you the book "The Giving Tree" by Shel Silverstein. I know this doesn't sound like much, but the story it tells resonates a message for you that I will live my life by. On the inside cover, I wrote this to you:

Punkin,

This was one of my most favorite books growing up, and I hope it becomes one of yours as well.

Let this story be a constant reminder of my unconditional love for you. No matter where you go or what you decide to do, always remember I will give everything that I am, simply to make you happy.

With all my heart and with all my life,

I love you.
Daddy

February 20, 2015

I can still say I literally have no idea what I'm doing. Mommy is going to the store to pick up the necessities, so I'm here with you for at least the next couple hours. I've gotten better, but I still get that twinge of panic in my stomach. She walks out the door, and you immediately begin bawling. CRAP! You've gotten into the terrible habit of only being comforted when I'm standing and holding you. I try to sit down real slow, slinking into the couch like a slug in slow motion, but some trigger in your brain goes off, and realize that I'm getting comfortable and you lose your mind. So what do I do? Do I just try to comfort you while I sit, knowing that I shouldn't give in to you, so that you're not completely spoiled? Well no! I end up pacing the house aimlessly for the next hour, wearing my feet to bloody nubs and the carpet to threads. At least the step counter on my new 'Fitbit' is setting record numbers.

You're growing so fast, that we're now in the panic "SHE MUST WEAR EVERYTHING SHE HASN'T WORN AT LEAST ONCE BEFORE IT DOESN'T FIT!" mode. There are days you are dressed up in three different cute outfits, with no intention of leaving the house to show them off, simply to get at least one picture of you in them. It's exhausting. We dressed you in a Supergirl outfit yesterday, which was adorable, but only for the few minutes you wore it for the necessary photo op and Facebook post.

> *"Listen earnestly to anything your children want to tell you, no matter what. If you don't listen eagerly to the little stuff when they are little, they won't tell you the big stuff when they are big, because to them all of it has always been big stuff."*
> —Catherine M. Wallace

A BRAND NEW YEAR

February 21, 2015

So let me just take a moment to list a couple of my most terrifying things I've encountered during the last 3 months. I always knew it would be difficult and strange, but no one ever mentioned the fact that there are things that could literally have a place in the next Steven King flick.

I may have mentioned it before, but it's obviously worth repeating. When you were born, I half expected to hear the doctor yell, "We need a comb in here, STAT!" During your first bath, the nurse literally tried (as well as several other unfortunate individuals who shall remain nameless) to wipe the dirt or poop off the bottom of your back. This wasn't either. It was hair. Dark, thick, dad-like back hair. You had low back hair that deserved a beret. Oh, it may be cute right now, but I was terrified, only seeing 18 years into the future with my daughter at the pool, sporting her backfro (back afro for you slow ones).

Your eyes are beautiful. They are kind of light, which makes me think they'll take after mine (not deep poop-brown like your mommy's). But there are times when the mechanics are just…off. One will be staring right at me, while the other seemed to take a mini vacation, veering off to stare at the TV or the random spot on the wall you love so much. I have this vision of your head starting to spin around, with your eyes rolling around in your head like a couple marbles. At other times, you suddenly go full-on cross-eyed, like I used to do when I was trying to squeeze a chuckle out of *my* dad; but I was 8. You have no idea you're being funny, as I laugh at you. But after a few seconds, I intentionally try to make them uncross, terrified they'll stick that way.

One last item and I'll try to lay off of the things that my perfect daughter does that makes me cringe. I was sitting on the couch yesterday staring at you, when I suddenly realized I was holding an alien. I could see your heartbeat. No, not from your chest, like one would assume, but from your *head*. Your soft spot was pulsing, so much so that I was sure at any moment it would burst and spray me. I imagined trying to plea my case to the cops, "I swear, officer, her head just exploded! I was just sitting there innocently!" Yes, I realize why it's there, and your mommy's private pieces thank you, but I still find it quite unsettling that the most important organ of your body is barely covered with a thin layer of membrane. I quickly put a hat on you, telling mom that your head was cold.

> *"The greatest mark of a father is how he treats his children when no one is looking."*
> —Dan Pearce

February 22, 2015

Your baby dedication was supposed to be today in Salem, but thanks to the crappy weather in Misery (Missouri is considered an optional spelling), we had to postpone. We decided to feed you cereal yesterday for the first time, and as with all firsts this year, it was an event. Mommy got your highchair all ready, and mixed the food powder with a dash of boob juice. It looked like a bowl of snot. I would love to say you did great, but I can't in good conscious lie to you. Once again, your tongue was the guilty party, popping in and out of your mouth like a piston trying to fire. If a molecule of food happened to make its way past the mouth threshold, it would quickly be shot back outside by the mouth muscle. It was a great success (and by success, I mean the dog ate like the Queen of England).

I got up with you this morning at around 2:00 for the graveyard feeding. I've now figured out that I need to change your diaper prior to feeding you, because that much jostling afterwards turns any oral intake quickly into oral outtake. I got you changed, onesie buttoned back up, and fed. I then sat you on my leg for the necessary burping session, but you would NOT relax your legs down, all curled up to your chest in some show of resistance to your master. I couldn't burp you like this, and was getting extremely flustered.

When I laid you down and noticed your appendages remained all contracted, I noticed that I had missed about 3 buttons in my drunken sleep state, thus causing your legs' awkward contortion. I despise buttons with a glowing passion. If you ever have a baby shower and happen to open a gift with a buttoned onesie inside: quietly go outside, set it aflame, and bury its miserable ashes in the name of your father's lost sanity. I'm writing the Dean at Missouri S&T requesting a class on onesie button snapping, the instructor requiring a minimum of a Doctorate in Physics and a Master's in Fabrics.

You always sleep on your stomach; never on your back (an audible gasp heard from the Mother's for Babies Safety Organization). We try to lay you quietly on your back when you've finally fallen asleep (after walking the hourly 5K for some unknown charity around the house), but as you drift further into dreamland – every time – your arms end up falling to the bed; scaring you awake into an "Arm Cut Off" level of screaming. So we don't even bother anymore. The only thing bad about this (besides the possibility of that small SIDS thing) is that you inevitably lose your pacifier somewhere in the night, and end up cramming it into your soft little check, placing the incriminating evidence of a half-nummy mark engraved into your face – a billboard to the world that we allow the unmentionable belly sleeping.

I also stay in a haze of amazement on how much you move. It seems like every muscle in your body is constantly firing, like they were dipped in liquid cocaine when I wasn't looking. Your head flips back and forth like you're at the Wimbledon tennis tournament and your arms like you're conducting some imaginary orchestra. I recently tried to put a straw in your hands and video you, so I could place it to some

Beethoven piece, but I couldn't find a wig small enough (and I'm not going to those measures for something of such potential hilarity without the corresponding head wear).

> *"He didn't tell me how to live; he lived,*
> *and let me watch him do it."*
> —Clarence Budington Kelland

February 26, 2015

I'm not quite sure how to go about training you. While talking to mommy on the phone today when she was at work, she left me with a task: "Practice rolling over with her." I sat in the floor of your room and stared at you. Practice rolling over?! I have a dog that *still* craps under the dining room table, and yet I've had the responsibility of teaching you your first party trick. The weight of this is immeasurable. I beseech the gods that I succeed better than I did with my talentless wiener dog, or else you'll be under that same dining room table with Evie 20 years from now, sniffing each other's butts.

I was told the proper way to go about the training the evening before. "Okay, make sure the arm that is corresponding to the side on which the roll will occur is flat on the lateral aspect of her auxiliary region…" Mommy had apparently done some homework on thebabywhisperer.com. I knelt next to you, and tried to replay the daunting process Mommy had laid out for me in my mind. I began flipping you back to front like a disabled gymnast for what felt like 4 days, and with each flip yelled, "YAAAY! WHAT A GOOD GIRL! YOU DID SO GOOD!!" as if you were helping with any part of the process. I felt like I should be

A BRAND NEW YEAR

shoving a Scooby Snack in your mouth for a reward. What do I reward a baby with for a job well done? Should I be placing a drop of breast milk on your tongue for each successful roll?

I'm slowly perfecting the "Putting the Baby to Sleep" ordeal. And by perfecting, I of course mean I've mastered the art of patting. I will never understand how this is what we've found over the last million years to be the sleep maker. If I was trying to go to sleep and someone was keeping beat on my back, I would eventually end up hanging myself – at least then I'd actually be sleeping. There are mechanisms of torture in place today (somewhere in Russia, if I was guessing) using this same technique on prisoners, and yet – it moves you to glorious unconsciousness. But I've become a pro, never the less. Sometimes, I get bored with the same routine, and spice it up, seeing if you can guess the tune I'm tapping out. You've never guessed right. Not even once. You didn't even get THIS one: TAP TAP TAP, TAP TAP TAP, TAP TAP TAP TAP TAP. It was Jingle Bells! Ugh, you're about as terrible at this game as you are at rolling over, but we'll work on it. Yesterday, I was holding Evie, and realized I was patting her back. She was looking at me with eyes that said, "Umm, what the heck are you doing?"

The hardest part I've found is not the *putting* you to sleep, but the *transferring* after you're asleep to be the upmost challenge. It's an impossible two-parter. First, getting up from wherever I'm sitting, and second laying you down – all while trying not to scare the diaper off you, which doesn't take much. Both parts must be completely fluid, with absolutely no jerks or hesitancy. If I make even one minor mistake, you flail your arms open, as if you just leapt off a bridge to bungee jump – managing to scare yourself awake, and thus starting the whole process over.

> "*Raising a child whether yours or not, is being anointed or chosen by God to be the guardian of his kingdom in a form of a child.*"
> —Unarine Ramaru

March 3, 2015

"And the Heavens opened and the angels proclaimed, 'Let us rejoice this blessed and glorious day, and remember the mercy the Lord has given to us, for on this day Kinley Marie, of the house McDonald, has slept through the night!'" It's a miracle! You went to bed last night at 9:00 and woke up at 7:00! I couldn't believe it. I woke up at 5:00, thinking that surely your mom feed you at your normal 2 am spot, but NO! I kept going in for the next couple hours to make sure you were alive and breathing.

And as if that wasn't enough beautiful news for one day, you pooped! It was an impressive load, and I've learned to make a mental note of the consistency and color of the production, because your mother apparently is keeping a diary of the poopy details. The conversation usually goes like this:

Me: "Hey babe, Kinley pooped today!"

Mommy: "Awesome! What color was it?"

Me: "Oh, um…green?"

Mommy: "Green?! Well, what shade of green? St. Patrick green? Money green? Neon lime green? Envy green? Harlequin mint grass green? "

Me: "Geez, I don't know, Michelangelo. What do I look like, a color wheel? I guess kind of a brownish green?"

Mommy: "Ugh, okay. So what was the consistency?"

Me: "Consistency?! So, I'm a chemist now? Should I have sent a sample to the lab??"

Mommy: "Do you have any idea what the consistency could mean?! Was it stringy?"

Me: "Stringy?!? What, like were there party favors in her poop?!"

This usually goes on for a couple hours. I've thought about taking pictures of them from now on, but something about that seems wrong, for some reason. I could see us innocently sitting around looking at old photo albums some day with your fiancé on Christmas Eve, accidentally come across the dookie album, and your man runs out of the house screaming in terror.

The drastic increase in the amount that you're eating is slightly frightening. I have this fear that during your 19th bottle of the day, your buttons will begin to pop open, and I'll look down and be holding a miniature female version of Augustus Gloop from Charlie and the Chocolate factory- as I'm sure you're dreaming of a flowing river of breast milk that you could fall into.

My favorite part of the feeding process is the burping. I am a man. Men like to do things that bring results for the hard work we put in. When I'm patting out the Star Spangled Banner rhythm on your back, and you give up the burp, I feel accomplished. It's the only thing in this whole baby process that gives me a reward. I should have a trophy made, but I have no idea what might go on top. Maybe, like the Kiss band's logo, or something? Or a bruised hand? I'm going to have to think about this one, and I'll get back to you.

"This parenting this is so easy!"
—No Parent Ever

PART 6

My Spring Chicken

March 11, 2015

"AND THE CROWD GOES WILD!" I felt like the father of an Olympian today that just won a gold medal. The gold medal in rolling over! Well, okay so maybe not the *gold* medal, because you only did it twice and it was actually pretty sloppy. The dismount was atrocious. I jumped up and cheered, your mom jumped up and cheered and then cried. It seems as though your mom can't fully enjoy any moment with mere happiness without underlying sadness, because it constantly reminds her that you're growth is inevitable.

You're now set on a strict routine, and if anyone tries to mess it up, they end up facing the Mothers Wrath. You need to eat at around 6:00 at night, so that we can feed you your last bottle at 9 in attempt for you to sleep through the night like a normal human. Your mother and I came home from work this week and your Nonni had put you to bed at 6. Your mother lost her mind, "DO YOU HAVE ANY IDEA WHAT YOU'VE DONE?!?"

If you happen to go to sleep too early, the whole night's jacked up. You have also become an infantile princess, making sure everyone in a 10 mile radius understands that it's your way or the highway. We just sat down to eat? Oh, well you're hungry now. I'm dog tired from working? You demand to be walked incessantly. We just rented a movie? You want to practice your screaming opera. Our world literally revolves around your plans and desires!

You are now a world-class finger sucker, to the point that the pacifier is useless. You go to town on your fingers to the point that I expect to pull your hand out and see the skeleton. I should probably go ahead and put a down payment at Dr. Harrison's office for your future braces and headgear, due to the fact that your teeth are likely to come out parallel to your nose.

Raising babies, I found, is actually just a real life version of Goldilocks. Everything has to be just right, or you'll end up being eaten by bears, or something. The bottle can't be too hot or too cold, just right. The bath water can't be too hot or too cold, just right. The baby room can't be too hot or too cold, just right. The baby mattress can't be too hard or too soft, you can't rock them too fast or too slow, the room can't be too bright or too dark, and the TV can't be too loud or too quiet. The pressure is surreal, because one mistake and I've served you up as bear food (at least that's how your mommy sees it).

One huge mistake I've made this week is finding out that we have a baby channel on TV. I'm sorry that I probably won't be around much longer, because I'm confident these shows are giving me terminal brain cancer. I can handle the kid's cartoons (SpongeBob is actually pretty awesome), but this is a whole different league. None of the characters ever really talk; it's just mind numbing gibberish ("goo goo, gaa gaa, blibble blabble, coo caw). And the colors are so bright and flashy, I expect for mommy to come home to me one day in a full blown, peed in my pants, mouth-foaming seizure.

You were a top-of-the-line crabby patty today. We had come to our wits end and decided to drive around - which is usually our last ditch effort to shut your trap. It worked. Well, it worked until we come to that stupid law of having to stop at red lights. There's some sort of wiring in your brain that signals your voice box to begin screaming in the chance your body stops moving for 2 seconds. So, in order to keep your majesty happy, I had to stop 10 yards before the car in front of me at any red light, and pump my brakes to keep the car rocking until it eventually turned green again. I'm sure everyone around me thought I had Parkinson's.

I wish I had every dollar I've spent on baby books and toys back so that I could do something more useful with it, like sprinkle them on the yard and mow over them to make mulch for the flower beds. I could literally dangle a used tissue in front of your face and you'd appreciate it as much as the necessary plastic ring of keys. And yet, we continue to buy it all. You already have more books in your possession than your mom's read in her lifetime (this is no joke). The crappy part about having all these books is that I really want to read them. I sit down with you and begin *The Bernstein Bears- Trouble at School* and you're screaming halfway through (again the brain wiring was triggered when you stopped moving). I end up feeling like a moron when I'm itching for you to finally go to bed so I can find out what happened after Brother Bear failed his quiz.

You have a house full of "baby toys" that I need to take to Goodwill as soon as your mother turns her back for a second. The house has suddenly become so crowded. It's as if mommy went through the house when you were born and said, "Oh, there's an empty square foot right there! That spot could use another swing! Is this couch really necessary here? How about we have three different kinds of insanely large jumpy things in its place?!"

I try desperately to make you enjoy them. I put you down in this huge round bouncing contraption with a table of toys around you. This stupid thing sucks for several reasons. I always end up getting a leg sideways by missing a hole while putting you down in it – this sends you over the edge like I had broken it off at the hip. Then, since you're too small for it right now, I have to pack 7 blankets around you so that when you do your normal weirdo head-dive you don't bust your face open. Finally, when I get you all in and ready to play, you're tired of it and ready to get out – which takes another 20 minutes because a 3 inch long foot is impossible to get out of a thigh sized hole when the baby is thrashing it about like a lunatic.

> *"Everyone should have kids. They are the greatest joy in the world. But they are also terrorists. You'll realize this as soon as they are born and they start using sleep deprivation to torture you."*
> —Ray Romano

March 15, 2015

We were finally both off on a Sunday and were able attend church together for the first time as a family. They had recently renovated the entire church, so you of course decided to christen the brand new carpet with a pile of milk vomit a mere two steps into the sanctuary. (I mashed it into the carpet with my foot when no one was watching).

As I sat there with my mom and dad on my left, and you and your mommy on my right, I was overwhelmed with emotion. My parents raised me in this church to know and love God. I've shed tears of happiness and grief around the alters, attended weddings and funerals, and experienced countless highs and lows. Many have grown old, moved away, moved back, had children, and had grandchildren. While here we have went through job changes, divorces, graduations, promotions, tragedies, successes, failures, and joy. But…through it all; God never changed.

I sat holding you and experiencing for the first time a mere glimpse of the depth of love God has for me and for you. My love for you is undying and deep, yet the love of God makes mine sink into the shadows. You need to understand this love, and understand it early. You will see how much I love you throughout your life, as evidenced by birthday gifts, hugs and kisses, and my frequent words of encouragement and inspiration. But God, through his love for you, gave you everything.

How can the baby doll I get you compare to the sunrise that he offers up? Could my simple words of, "I've loved you since the moment you were born" ever possibly compare to his words of, "I've loved before anything that is- ever was." No matter how close I get to you, He will always be closer. Yes, I'm your daddy, but only because your forever-daddy has entrusted you to me for a short while. It's up to me to not let him down on how I raise his beautiful baby girl.

God is your biggest fan. His love for you doesn't grow the more perfectly you live, and it doesn't lessen with all the mistakes you'll make.

Look into the stands: that's God cheering you on, waving a foam finger saying that YOU are his number one. Look past the finish line: that's God screaming in excitement and pride, ready to tackle you with joy and hoist you onto his shoulders for a victory lap. Listen for him in the bleachers, shouting and chanting your name, starting the wave in your honor. God will always be on your side and in your corner. Everything I could do for you, He will always do much more.

He's wearing a t-shirt that says, "Man, I really LOVE this girl!!" with an arrow pointing to you. If he drinks coffee in Heaven, it says, "World's Proudest Dad". He signs all his letters to you "Love, Your BFF." He's placed your picture next to his bed, on his keychain, on the dash of his car. Your face is his computer's background, and his phone's screensaver, constantly fishing it out to show off his kid to any angel who happens to pass the throne. He's all about you and can't get enough of you.

> *"Children who have faith have distinctly different characteristics from those who don't. In fact, one of the main manifestations of a person with strong faith is the ability to give—not just in terms of money or possessions, but also time, love, and encouragement."*
> —Stormie Omartian

March 20, 2015

We took you for your 4 month appointment today to get your second round of shots. The first round actually went really well, and you didn't cry much at all. This time was different. You've now developed a personality, so you smile when you're happy, pout when you're sad, and you have this specific one-of-a-kind cry when you're hurt. It's become my least favorite sound in the world.

The second the needle broke the skin, your eyes shot wide and your mouth shot open- with that cry. That heart-breaking "how-could-you-let-them-do-this-to-me" cry. I pulled you up in my arms and kept whispering in your ear that it would be okay. My most important job as your daddy is to shield from you anything that could possibly hurt. But, I'm so sorry to say, that I won't always be able to do that. You will be hurt in life.

I remember my first day of school. I was a nervous wreck. Oh, don't get me wrong, I was completely equipped for the day! Pound Puppies backpack with matching trapper keeper, pencils, art box, and a shiny apple for Ms. Kazmeric. Although I had everything I needed to succeed, my stomach still turned when your Mema woke me up to cart me off to my brand new adventure. I had no idea what I was in store for. Would every student get a "spanking" on the first day? I'd been warned about that spanking business. What if they only served broccoli for lunch? What then?! As Mema dropped me off, and noticed the mist beginning in the corners of my eyes, she's whispered a simple, "Gavin, it's going to be okay."

I've had countless instances in this life where I've faced what I was sure was a losing battle. Being dropped in Phoenix at 18 years old, having never lived on my own. Being made to resign my church in Illinois after I was sure it was where God wanted me. Losing jobs. Losing a wife. Losing people I loved with everything I had. No wonder I feel like a loser. So many times I've sat in front of my parents on the couch in their living room, with my heart crushed, feeling completely lost in life, not knowing whether I would be able to endure another blow. But in the middle of every circumstance, after the tears had turned my eyes red once again, my dad continues to smile at me with those "Trust me" eyes of his, and I know what he's about to say. "It's all going to be okay."

What are you facing right now that may be causing you pain? As you get older, there may be a doctor's report that frightens you. You may find yourself drowning in bills, feeling like you'll never dig out. People you love may meet our God before you had a chance to say what you always wanted to say. You may someday have a job on the brink, or a marriage on the rocks. You will probably have someone you love break your heart. You could even come to a point where you sit in your empty house night after night, feeling so completely lonely, as if the weight of the house was on your chest.

I'm sitting here after your shots, looking at your tear stained face and doing my absolute best to ease your pain. But Punkin, you must understand that I won't always be around. Feel free to cry to God. Feel free to sit in his living room and vent. I can imagine what his response will be. Just like the father at the basketball game. You've just missed the winning shot, and he walks you back to the locker room with his strong arm around your shoulder. You proceed to tell him all the reasons why you're a failure, and he will remind you of all the reasons why you're a champion.

Trust me, your heart is not the only one breaking. Crawl up into his lap and bury your face into his neck, as he rocks back and forth. Through a cracking voice and his own misting eyes, he will once again tell you, "Baby… Sweetie, look at me. Listen to me. Are you listening? It's going to be okay…. It's going to be okay."

"What God is to the world, parents are to their children."
—Philo

March 23, 2015

Well, the days of simple feedings are over. The doctor has suggested to begin adding this infant oatmeal stuff to your bottles and to also start occasional cereal feedings from the bowl. In addition to this, Kylie wants to replace one or two of your daily bottles for formula, since her boobie milk supply is running low. I had no idea this was going to be so difficult. You're a baby, and the instructions for feeding now make me want to call Chef Boyardee for advice.

No, but seriously: The formula requires special water you must use and then you half the amount of water used to find the amount of scoops to add. The oatmeal is added to breast milk, and you use 1/3 teaspoons to the amount of milk. If you do bowl cereal, it's pretty much a guessing game of adding milk to powder to eventually arrive at the correct consistency. This has been my hardest to master. It always turns out either straight liquid like I've added nothing at all, or thick as paste.

When I finally get the impossible spoon feeding consistency, I have enough cereal for you, me, mommy, Evie, and every other baby in a 25 mile radius. I inevitably end up standing in the kitchen, staring cross-eyed at all the possibilities, and wishing I could just make you a ham sandwich. This morning I decided to make an oatmeal and milk bottle in advance, because I think I'm smart or something, and ended up also adding cereal to it later. I couldn't understand why you were having such a hard time with it, until I realized I had a bottle of hardened cement.

I also never realized that the hole in the stinking nipples come in a billion different diameters, lengths, parsecs, and depths. I went to feed you this afternoon, and your cheeks were sucking in like you were trying to get chocolate malt through a coffee stirrer, to the point I'm going to have to explain the busted blood vessels in your eyes to your mom when she gets home. I realized the hole was too small for the now thickened meals, so I cut a miniscule slit in the top. Well, then I might as well have opened the bottle and splashed it onto your face. You were coughing and gagging like I'd dipped you head first in your own private vat of breast milk. Plus, every 3 seconds, I have to stop and mash the nipple since I apparently never seem to shake it enough; there's always a mound of undissolved powder impeding the flow.

> *"In spite of the six thousand manuals on child raising in the bookstores, child raising is still a dark continent and no one really knows anything. You just need a lot of love and luck – and, of course, courage."*
> —Bill Cosby

March 24, 2015

It's the first big storm of Spring, and it's turning into a doosie. With each flash of lightening, I quickly try to cover your ears, knowing a deafening thunder clap is close behind. You're scared to death, but I'm loving every second. When I was young, I was terrified of storms. Anytime that heart-stopping beep started on the television set, I was ready to pack up every Lego and He-Man action figure, and head to the basement for a few weeks. One bolt of lightning, I was bawling. A window-shaking roll of thunder, and I was screaming for Dad to hurry up. He would slowly get himself off the couch, and lead all of us down to safety. How could he be this calm, when Hurricane I'm-Going-To-Kill-You is knocking on our front door?! Did he not care at all?! Of course he did. It's just that he had a different perspective.

When a child sees a storm, Dad just saw a great spring shower. He had been around long enough to know that these things pass. So had Jesus. The very storm that made the disciples shake in their robes, made Jesus drowsy. When the disciples were pulling their hair out in fear, Jesus was a calm cucumber. How on Earth could he sleep through such a storm? Easy, he was in charge of it.

You will eventually face storms that will scare the life out of you. But never forget who you have on your side, who you have playing on your team, who you have hiding in the bottom of your boat. In HIS timing, not your own, he will look straight at your reeling waves and simply say, "Okay, it's time to be quiet. She's endured enough of the storm. She deserves some peace." Just like your earthly Father, your heavenly Father knows the storm you're in right now will also eventually pass. You will soon learn to enjoy your personal storms, because it's just another chance to see God to show off. But don't you worry, Punkin, I'll continue to hold your ears until this storm passes. You're still my baby, so there's no need to be facing storms alone just yet.

> *"A child needs both to be hugged and unhugged. The hug lets her know she is valuable. The unhug lets her know that she is viable. If you're always shoving your child away, they will cling to you for love. If you're always holding them closer, they will cling to you for fear."*
> —Polly Berrien Berends

March 28, 2015

I'm completely falling apart. It's like the second I became a dad, my body said, "Welp, guess it's time to start deteriorating everywhere." I waited a long time to have babies, so I'm not as spry as the other dads on the block. My low back has recently begun to throb and burn if I even think about moving. I stay in this constant haze of sleepiness and find myself staring half eyed at nothing in particular with my mouth gaped open multiple times a day. The bags under my eyes are big enough to pack them for vacation, and for some reason my complexion has reverted to my 15-year-old 'Stride' stage. I could probably walk barefoot on hot coals at this point due to my calloused soles on account of the constant walking with you. I'm quickly taking on the hearing of a dead mole, the vision of a headless bat, and the memory of a flushed goldfish.

I'm losing what little hair I have left so fast that I'm convinced some jerk snuck into my shower and switched my shampoo with Nair. I've found this brown powder stuff that I sprinkle on my hair to help cover up the really thin places, but you puked on my head the other day and I ended up having black streaks running down my face: looked like a crying girl whose mascara was running. I have this deep fear that one of your best friends will come over to the house and say, "Oh, I didn't know you lived with your grandpa." Then I'll end up having to forbid you from ever hanging out with that stupid girl again.

I bought this insanely tight undershirt girdle thingy the other day that you wear to suck all your fat in and help smooth out the escaping rolls. It works okay, but it makes me so uncomfortable that I end up walking as if I'm trying out for the lead in Frankenstein, and it rubs my nips so raw I'm forced to put Band-Aids over them for the next two days.

Well, I think I've embarrassed myself enough for one day. The one thing that is good about all this is that I'm slowly beginning to actually look like an old father. I guess it's probably a good thing, or else when you're older, your friends will think I'm your brother and start hitting on me. I have a feeling your mommy wouldn't care too much for that.

"The value of marriage is not that adults produce children, but that children produce adults."
—Peter De Vries

March 30, 2015

I took care of a very sick little girl today at work. She was one of the sweetest, most polite and considerate girls I've ever taken care of. Many people would look at this girl and think "She's different". Or they might say, "Aww, that's too bad. I feel so sorry for her", because the thing was: she had Down Syndrome. When I found out her condition, I did not want to take care of her. I knew her kind would be on the call light incessantly. She would be much more work, and would need a lot more attention and care than I wanted to give today. But then my whole world was turned upside down... She loved me. She had never met me before in her life, but because I showed her compassion and care, she loved me. Anytime she would need something, she would holler, "Davin! Davin, come weally fast, I need you!"

When I ran to her room for possibly the hundredth time, she was crying and saying, "I need to potty!! I need to potty!" She was too weak to walk, so I picked her up and began running to the bathroom. Half way there she began saying, "I'm having an accident, Davin!" and I glanced back to see the trail of urine on the floor and soaked into my scrubs. I got her to the restroom, and proceeded to change her out of the dirty gown in place of a clean one, and decided to wash the vomit out of her hair.

Half way through, she began crying again. She looked up to me through tear-filled eyes and began repeating, "Davin, I'm so sowry. I'm so so sowry. I messed up your scwubs. I'm so sowry." The biggest lump began to rise in my throat, to the point of almost overflowing with emotion. Through a cracking voice, I whispered, "Sweetie, I don't care about by scrubs. When they're dirty, I know I did my job in taking care of you!" I loved her. Like her love for someone she's never met, I in turn loved her.

Princess, remember that you can never judge anyone on what your eyes tell you. Our eyes have a terrible reputation for labeling people in the completely wrong way. When I first saw this little girl, I immediately began to think along with what my eyes were telling me. I felt sorry for her. I felt sorry for her parents. I felt sorry for how her life would be filled with hard times and difficult situations. But God put her there today to punch me in the gut. She should have been the one feeling sorry for me. She should have felt sorry for my quick assumptions of character based on my lying eyes. I was a fool.

When you were born, I was so happy that you were "normal". And by normal, you didn't have any fingers or toes missing, you didn't have a weird mutation, a cleft lip, a chromosomal abnormality, anything. In my *eyes* you were perfect. But remember, to God that little girl is perfect.

The Bible says that we look at the outward appearance, but God looks at the heart. You will end up coming across people in your life that may look different than you, they may not be as smart or as pretty, but just remember that you can never trust your eyes, you can only trust God's.

This perfect little girl also reminded me of God's unconditional compassion for us. He is the nurse that will come running to your bedside the minute you need him. He is the one that will carry you to the bathroom when you've made a mess of your life. He will exchange your soiled heart with a clean one, wash the junk out of your mind, and wipe up the trail of tears you've left down the hall. We always end up saying the same thing, "God, I'm so sorry. I'm so, so sorry. I've messed up your robe." God will look back at you with those same tear-filled eyes and say, "Sweetie, I don't care about my robe! When they're dirty, I know I did my job in taking care of you!"

You will someday find yourself in need of some intensive care. You will be lying on a stretcher of misfortune and bad luck. You may have been admitted for shameful sins, stupid mistakes, or deep depression. But keep in mind that God is the ultimate care giver. You may not always be able to see him at your bedside, but the call light is always there.

"It's not our job to toughen our children up to face a cruel and heartless world. It's our job to raise children who will make the world a little less cruel and heartless."
—L.R. Knost

PART 7

So Many Plans

April 2, 2015

For the last 5 months, every time I would think of something I wanted us to do together, I would jot it down in my phone to remember later. I've compiled quite the list, and should probably go ahead and write them here. At this point, we have plenty on our bucket lists to last us until your grandchildren are born. Here's what all I plan to do in the next several years:

- ✓ Use your baby cuteness at a Cardinals game, make a "My First Game" sign, and hopefully get us a free ball or autograph.
- ✓ Put all our covers on the living room floor for our very own Sleepover. You can even choose the movie.
- ✓ I'll brush your hair whenever you ask. I'll even let you brush what little I'll have left. There will come a day when you won't want to.
- ✓ Give you Hollywood level voices to all the characters in the books I will read to you.
- ✓ I'll praise you for your barely tinted Easter egg that you couldn't let soak for more than a few seconds. Then I'll "hide" those almost white eggs around the living room, and gawk at amazement that

you found them all- even though I can easily see every one of them from my place on the couch.
- ✓ Show you how to safely handle and dispose of a sparkler so that you don't end up a ball of fire and will have to come visit Daddy in the ER.
- ✓ Take you to the store to secretly buy Mommy a very special Mother's Day gift that you'll pick out all by yourself. Oh, and help you make a macaroni necklace to go with it, of course.
- ✓ Let you ride on my shoulders, on my back, on top of my feet. Where ever you want for as long as you want. Before I know it, you'll be too big.
- ✓ You can give me a makeover. Just don't tell Mommy that we're using her "good" stuff. It's apparently pretty expensive.
- ✓ Teach you the *correct* way to tie your shoes. None of that rabbit around the tree junk.
- ✓ I'll learn all the new and stylish ways to braid hair, so I can help when Mommy's at work.
- ✓ Go to the zoo. We'll laugh at the size of the elephant's poop, while Mommy rolls her eyes at us. Then we'll scare her by pretending I dropped you in the lion's den.
- ✓ Stare in amazement at the "Picasso" style face you've carved into the miniature pumpkin. And again, teach you how to avoid going to Daddy's work.
- ✓ Kiss you good morning every morning. Kiss you good night every night.
- ✓ Lie on a blanket in the back yard at night and show you how to find the big dipper.
- ✓ Buy you a doll, and then another doll. And yet, more dolls. Even though I don't understand it, I realize a little girl can't have too many dolls.

- ✓ Introduce you to classic movies I loved as a kid like The Sandlot, Three Ninja's, Snoopy Come Home, Follow That Bird, and The Reluctant Dragon.
- ✓ Introduce you to the classic books I loved as a kid like The Giving Tree, The Best Nest, Wacky Wednesday, I Wish That I Had Duck Feet, Where the Sidewalk Ends, and Fox in Socks.
- ✓ Attempt heart shaped pancakes on Valentine's morning.
- ✓ Hide black eyed peas in your mashed potatoes on New Year's Day so that you may have 12 months of good luck. Unless by some weird chance you'll actually like black eyed peas, then I won't have to hide them. My grandma always had to hide mine.
- ✓ Put princess Band-Aids on every cut, scratch, and red mark you happen to find on your body that you think is killing you.
- ✓ Point at every red light at the top of radio towers on the way home from Mema and Papaw's on Christmas Eve, and convince you it's Rudolf.
- ✓ Take you to the movies. I won't make a big deal that you want to bring a doll along too.
- ✓ Put your drawings on my desk at work. Yes, they'll be all over the refrigerator as well, but I'll want to show them off much more than in just the kitchen.
- ✓ Let you pick the radio station, even if it's that awful Kid's Bop stuff. I'll even sing along with you at the top of my lungs. We won't ask Mommy to sing along…you'll soon realize out why… ouch.
- ✓ Get all dramatic with fake choking every time we're around someone that's smoking, in hopes you grow up knowing how bad it is for you.
- ✓ You will eventually find a random animal that you'll bring home as a pet. I'll cut the holes in the top of the box and run to the store for some carrots to cut up.

SO MANY PLANS

- ✓ Laugh at every joke you tell me, even if it has no actual point: "Daddy, you know why the hippo ate his poop? Because the squirrel was too busy!!" Me: "BWAAAHAHAHA!!!"
- ✓ I'll nibble on whatever you bring me made out of Play-Doe, and pretend it's the most amazing thing I've ever put in my mouth.
- ✓ Dance with you. Now when you're a baby, and later when you're a woman. I'll dance with you whenever you'll let me.
- ✓ Make sure we're watching the Thanksgiving Day Parade all the way to the end, so we can jump up and down at the *real* Santa Clause.
- ✓ Show up unexpectedly to your school during lunch with pizza for you and your friends.
- ✓ Buy you an umbrella so we can play in the rain. I'll take the heat from Mommy when we accidentally track in mud.
- ✓ Listen to every detail about your day when you come home from school.
- ✓ Paint your nails. I got a lot of practice on Mommy's toes while you were still in her belly. I gotta say, I didn't do half bad.
- ✓ Start a garden with you. Even though I won't eat any of those nasty veggies we'll grow. Maybe we can just have flowers.
- ✓ Make sure you're in the best position at local parades. The front row actually isn't the best. Right in front of the curb is where all the candy will come to rest. Trust me, we'll make a haul.
- ✓ Play basketball, hockey, baseball, and football, whatever sport you want. I guarantee you'll be better than me in all of them.
- ✓ Throw whatever kind of party you want for your birthday. You want a petting zoo? Check. A magician? You got it. A ferris wheel? A car full of clowns? No problem.
- ✓ Show you how to make a proper sundae. And don't worry about putting on too many sprinkles. I will probably have just as many on mine.

- ✓ Instruct you in the ways of cookie dunking. If your knuckles are dry, you're not doing it right.
- ✓ Take you to someplace out of town you've never been at least once a year.
- ✓ Show you how a boy is supposed to treat a girl by the way I treat your Mommy.
- ✓ Go sledding, build a snowman, make snow angels, drink hot chocolate with a questionably large amount of marshmallows, and make snow ice cream.
- ✓ Help you pick all the dandelions in the yard for a handmade bouquet for Mommy. Trust me, she will love it.
- ✓ Tell you how beautiful you are if you happen to get braces. If you feel bad about them, I'll show you a picture of me with mine. Yours could not *possibly* be worse.
- ✓ You will eventually learn all about sex, drugs, violence, and alcohol from television, movies, school, and friends. But I plan to teach you about all these things first.
- ✓ Take you to the beach. You can bury me in the sand and give me fake boobs. Trust me, I would expect nothing less, and will probably be laughing harder than you will be.
- ✓ Show you how to achieve the perfect browned marshmallow over a campfire. It's all about height and constant turning. Unless you take after Mema and want them charred to a black crisp.
- ✓ Let you choose your Halloween costume every year. Don't worry, I won't say anything if you're going as a princess…again…for the 6th year in a row. I'll dress up as Prince Charming.
- ✓ Help you write a letter to Santa every year. I'll get you special glitter pens and stickers to use, so we're sure that it *really* stands out from all the other kid's letters.
- ✓ Paint a flag on your cheek for the Fourth of July, an STL for Cardinals Games, a heart for Valentines, a dog paw for home football games, and even the occasional rainbow or sun for

random occasions. I'll be sure to always have plenty of face paint on hand.
- ✓ Never turn you down when you ask me to push you on the swing. There will come a day when you'll want to do it all by yourself.
- ✓ Help you with your homework. I won't give you the answers, but I'll show you how to do it.
- ✓ Make sure you experience the good old-time candies like Candy Buttons, Ring Pops, Nik L Nips, Pop Rocks, Sugar Daddy's, Mary Jane's, Peanut Butter Bars, and Bottle Caps.
- ✓ Always keep a picture of you in my wallet, and make sure you always have a picture of me to keep in your purse.
- ✓ Decorate Christmas cookies with you. No matter how good you think mine are, yours will always be better. Even if you iced the Santa cookie in green and added a mound of chocolate chips.
- ✓ Give you an allowance, but you will have to earn it by doing your chores. You will then be required to give 10% of that allowance back to God. Trust me on this one; you'll be blessed throughout your life.
- ✓ Eat breakfast together before school at the table, and then eat dinner together in the evenings at the table. This will be time we will cherish forever.
- ✓ Never, ever make fun of you.
- ✓ As hard as it will be, I'll let you stay overnight at your cousins house early in life. This will teach you independence, and make it easier to leave home for college. Easier for you *and* for us.
- ✓ Make sure you're cultured by taking you to the Symphony, the Opera, and the Theatre. I'll be going for the music, the acting, and the venues. You'll be going so you have an excuse to dress like a real princess in public.

- ✓ Show you the power of saying you're sorry. It's okay if you want to always have the last word, just make sure those words are an apology.
- ✓ Take you to Meramec Springs and see who can keep their feet in the ice cold water the longest. My dad would never let us off easy on this challenge, so you'll have to earn this win. Be warned, it may take several years for you to beat me. (A little secret, if you put your feet on the moss at the bottom, it helps.)
- ✓ Play games in the car. "In My World", "Snaps", and "I Spy" are a couple of my favorites. Picking an object during "I Spy" that was outside and we passed an hour ago is against the rules.
- ✓ Let you win at board games. Except for Candy Land. Candy Land is my jam. You'll have to earn that win. Wait… and Hi-Ho Cherry-O.

> *"Being a father is the most important role I will ever play and if I don't do this well, no other thing I do really matters."*
> —Unknown

April 3, 2015

I'm in terrible pain. I've never felt pain like this before, and between you and me, your Daddy doesn't handle pain very well. If I happen to stub my toe, you've have thought my leg had been bitten off by an alligator. My low back has been killing me lately, so after complaining and moaning for a few days straight, Mommy made me go to the doctor.

SO MANY PLANS

Partly because she was worried about me, but I'm sure mostly because she was tired of me acting like a baby (no offence).

I have this terrible fear that I'm going to go into the doctor some day for a mild problem and learn that I actually have Stage 12 brain/bowel/lung/bladder cancer and have 6 days to live. I was convinced that I have spine cancer, and your mom gets so mad at me every time I mention it. I had to have an MRI done, and was nervous to the point of making myself sick waiting for the results all day. Come to find out, I have a protruding disk with a tear and have to go to a back surgeon in Springfield. So not cancer, thank God. But I'm still in terrible pain that I would probably give a solid 7. I began to think about pain. Not the physical pain in my back, but the spiritual pain in my soul. I've messed up so much.

"What's your pain on a scale of 1 to 10, with 1 being very little pain to 10 being the worst you can imagine?" This is a question that I ask every patient, so that I know how much relief to provide. Usually, after medication is given, their pain number slowly beings to decline. But then there is something called Chronic Pain that many people deal with on a daily basis. This is pain that no matter what medication is given or relief measures taken, it's always there. Always nagging at you. Always hurting.

I hope you haven't found yourself in a place where you are dealing with chronic pain. Not pain in your joints from arthritis, or pain behind your eyes from a headache, but a deep burning pain in your heart. Pain from someone giving up on you. Pain from losing a job. From a dying loved one, a bad report from the doctor, a never-ending pile of bills, a lonely heart, a hurtful childhood, a seemingly futureless life. These things can grow to an unrelenting chronic pain in your soul. My pain today is a 7, but my chronic pain lately has been a 5. My heart is hurting, and I don't know how to find relief. I find myself broken from all the hard things that try to hurt us and bring us pain in life. You will face them too. And, like the rest of us, you too will experience pain.

WebMD tells us the number one way to decrease chronic pain: Breathe. Slow down, step back, and just breathe.

I remember when you were being born, and your Mommy was having a really hard time. The pain medication wasn't helping, the cool wash cloths and ice chips weren't helping, and me holding her hand wasn't helping. Then I saw the nurse practically crawl into bed with your mom, get right in her face, and began telling her, "Just breathe, Kylie. Just breathe with me."

That's where I am, and where you will find yourself someday. Does God take away the pain? No more than I could take away the pain your Mommy was feeling. I have one major job: to simply help her through it. Today, your heart may be crushed. You can't seem to focus. You want to throw in the towel, walk away, and quit. That's right when you'll find our God, kneeling down in front of you, blocking your exit. He takes your tear-stained face in his nail-pierced hands and whispers, "Punkin….just breathe, honey. Look into my eyes, and breathe with me. The pain is not forever. I promise. Just. Breathe."

> *"Where will our country find leaders with integrity, courage, strength—all the family values—in ten, twenty, or thirty years? The answer is that you are teaching them, loving them, and raising them right now."*
> —Barbara Bush

April 8, 2015

On Sunday morning, you woke early to find that the ole' Easter bunny had visited you! You must have sent him a letter directly without me knowing, because you got exactly what you were wanting: a pair of bunny ears, a couple new books, a sponge to play with in the bathtub, and a few teething toys. I was slightly disappointed you didn't get the 50 pound chocolate bunny I've had my eye on at Walmart, but maybe next year. That's daddy's kind of teething toy.

We dolled you up in your finest dress to date, and attended church with your Mema, Papaw, and cousins. Papaw played a judge in the Easter program that was weighing all the evidence of whether Jesus is truly God's son. I sure hope you know the story by now, but the evidence was clear. He is without a doubt.

It just so happens that this year on April 5th, 3 huge events took place on the same day: Easter Sunday, your mommy's birthday, and the Opening Day of Baseball. I usually go to the Opening Day game, but the Cardinals started the season on the road this year in Chicago (gross), so I decided to throw a party. A few days before the big game, I started decking the whole house out in Cardinal decorations. I even made baseball cupcakes and wrote a Cardinals Trivia game we could all play for prizes. For some reason I was singing Christmas carols while getting everything ready, and thought up an amazing new version to a classic. I have a feeling it will be known world-wide in just a few short days:

"It's beginning to look a lot like baseball,
Everywhere you go.
Take a look at the grass so green,
The balls so white and clean.
On clear blue nights
With big bright lights aglow!

It's beginning to look a lot like baseball,
Soon the fans will show.
And the prettiest sight to see,
Are the Cardinals that will be,
Champions once more!!!"

Your mom keeps saying, "Ugh, you're so obsessed!" I have a feeling she's a little sore I decided to put so much effort into a party on her birthday that actually had nothing to do with a party *for* her birthday. Think daddy may have messed up a little on that one. I told her that I had not gotten her anything for her birthday, since she refused to ask for anything specific, and insisted she just pick something out she wanted and buy it. (Yeah, not so personable there, moron.) When I realized that her feelings were actually pretty hurt, I felt terrible and decided to leave work early today and find something for her.

I ended up getting her some new running shoes, a gift certificate for the tanning salon, some new headbands, a watch, and made up one of those corny coupon books with things like "1 Hour Massage, Give the Dog a Bath, and One Night Sole Possession Of Remote" written on them. I felt stupid, but her expression was priceless. She loved it. Were the tennis shoes what her heart had been yearning after for years? I doubt it, but I finally saw how "It's the thought that counts" is surprisingly pretty accurate.

This reminded me of one of my fondest memories from a couple years ago. I made a huge discovery while mowing. I found a turtle in my yard. Now, I know this may seem like a small happening to you, but to your cousin Jake, it's was like Christmas came 6 months early. Jake has been obsessed with needing a turtle for months, so when I saw one lazily crawling in my backyard, I was ecstatic. I brought him in, and proceeded to transform an ordinary box into a private turtle condo, equipped with the necessary water bowl, grass, and apple slices (I had to Google what food they could eat).

We go to such extremes when searching for gifts for the ones we love, don't we? I've seen people stalking the malls, and roaming the aisles. I'm not describing the last-minute purchases of the Walgreens perfume by the front register in the plastic clam shell. Forget blue-light specials or Groupon deals; I'm talking about that love-filled gift for that very special person. Trust me, there's no greater feeling than seeing the one you love light up when they open your gift. Why do we do it?

Why did God do it? Why bless us with gifts that make our eyes pop, and our heart stop? He could easily be giving me a shack in Heaven, but he's building me a mansion. Why did he give the birds a song, mountains a peak? He could have easily made the sunset black and white. Why wrap creation in such amazing majesty? Why does he go to so much trouble to give us these gifts?

When Aunt Amy told me that she showed Jake the picture of the turtle saying it was for him, he said, "Holy cwap, you gotta be kidding me?!" Next time a sunset steals your breath or a meadow of flowers leaves you speechless, remain that way for a while. Say nothing and listen as God whispers, "Do you like it? I did it just for you." I'll probably give God the same response Jake gave.

> *"Let your eyes light up when your children are around. Laugh more. Tell them how empty and quiet it is when they're not there. Enjoy the things they bring to your life. Attend their activities, not as if they were compulsory for parents, but throw yourself into their lives."*
> —Valerie Bell

April 13, 2015

I've slowly begun to realize the hundreds of ways that a 10 pound infant can successfully injure an adult man. In the past couple weeks, you've managed in multiple ways to actually inflict harm upon me. I know the reason God gave us fingernails. They are just sharp enough to allow us to scratch various itching areas on our body without slicing through to the underlying muscle. And yet, I have a feeling you've handcrafted your own prison file under your mattress that you're using at night to file your nails to razor-thin width. Yesterday, I was playing with you when one of your hand daggers found my bottom lip. It quickly looked like I had tried to lick cake batter off of moving blender blades. A miniscule slice in my lip gushing blood as if I'd cut it completely off, all brought about by a nail the size of a half grain of rice.

I'm also convinced it's your upmost goal in life to knock me out completely with a genuine Hulk Hogan head butt. I never know when it's coming. There's no leading up to it, or any sort of warning signs given that a black eye for daddy is coming. I'll be holding you facing me, going through our normal sounds that make you laugh. In your mind, I'm sure it goes something like, "This is fun. I'm having a good time. Haha, that sound was funny. Yep, just hanging out with Dad. I'm kind of hungry. And… ALL MY NECK MUSCLES HAVE JUST LIQUIFIED!! NO CONTROL OF HEAD MOTION!! MUST THROW HEAD IN DIRECTION OF DADDY, HE'LL KNOW WHAT TO DO!!!"

Yes, I do know what to do. I'll just unknowingly place my fragile face in the tumultuous path of your plummeting head so it has a nice, soft place to land. It's seriously like a lightning bolt how fast it all happens. Your mommy is convinced all the little red marks on your forehead are from hitting it on the slats in your crib. If she would happen to look closer, she would quickly realize all those red marks have the shocking similarity and resemblance to the shape of DADDY'S TEETH.

I'm also amazed that a 6 month old has the arm strength and speed of a starting pitcher. You're now able to grasp your little toys enough that you can get them to your mouth for the obligatory sucking, or swing them wildly around as if the toy had suddenly and unpredictably caught fire and it's taped to your hand. None of your toys have any sort of metal, sharp edges, weigh more than 2 ounces, and yet when they suddenly come in contact with my temple, I half expect to look down and see you grasping an anvil.

You will also now go into these unpredictable fits of kicking that terrifies me. There will be nothing in particular happening to incite sudden overflowing happiness that could spread to your legs, but they suddenly remind me of seeing Grandma McDonald throw frog legs into the frying pan without cutting the tendon first. They go completely insane. You look exactly like mommy would if I secretly placed a tarantula on her foot, and she notices it a second later. It's so sudden and severe, that I jump out of my skin every time. You're not even half a year old yet, and determined to stop my heart. And on top of that, the leg kicks are powerful. I'm tempted to run by Lowe's, grab some boards, and place them at your feet to begin your martial arts training.

> *"No word makes me happier than the word "daddy" when it's directed to me."*
> —Michael Josephson

PART 8

Growing So Fast

April 16, 2015

We drove to St. Louis today simply to buy you more clothes, as you've suddenly decided that you want to pack on about a pound per day. I guess I never realized how quickly your sizes change. At this very moment, I'm wearing a t-shirt that I bought in high school (yes, it's slightly tight, but it's my day off so shut up). You're in one size at the beginning of dinner and then suddenly notice you're now in a new size bracket by dessert. Three to six months. Six to 9 months. 9 months to 12 months. They're making a fortune on us! I half expect on the next trip to see 7 months 2 weeks to 7 months 3 weeks, or 321 days to 323 days.

The only thing really bad about buying you new clothes (besides the fact that I'm running out of plasma to sell) is that your poor mother continues to be an ever-increasing ball of emotion with your growing. You've completely run out of space for clothes (can't imagine how something like that would happen), so we had to pack up everything that's now too small. While putting clothes into the storage bin, for some unknown idiotic reason, I had the audacity to suggest we donate the clothes to a local charity. You would have thought I suggested we pack you up with it, and ship you to Zimbabwe. "We are NEVER getting rid of these!! We'll want to go through them later so it will remind us of when she was younger!! What if we have another girl?! What if she wants to use them on her dolls?!" I had apparently made a huge mistake in the suggestion. I'm learning as I go.

Your poop routine has finally leveled out to some sort of pattern. We can expect a huge production every couple of days. The bad part is, since you're now eating green beans, the extent of stank has reached an all-time high. I deal with poop and vomit on a daily basis at work, but yours have recently begun to put them to shame. For the first time yesterday, I gagged. My eyes welled up with tears as I gagged and you laughed. I can say with all honesty that I use on average 12-14 wipes per poop. There are so many random creeks and crevices that the poop can travel to that I end up spending 30 minutes pulling apart leg rolls only to find more hiding.

Up to this point, I was convinced that the Diaper Genie was the greatest invention in the history of ever, but I'm quickly realizing that it hadn't met its match until now. With this new brand of poo, the thin plastic liners cannot compete with the hair curling fragrance. I keep waiting for the day when they come out with the steel plated liners. I should invent those. Dad's around the world would come together with joined hands around it singing like the Who's at the end of The Grinch That Stole Christmas.

"Everything depends on upbringing."
—Leo Tolstoy

April 17, 2015

Tonight I took you to Salem for the annual Miss Salem Pageant! Your great Aunt Belinda and Uncle Kelly came all the way from Carthage to see your cousin Natalie compete. Would you believe it, she won! I was ecstatic! I've always been such a huge supporter of Natty's.

A couple years ago, I showed up at Natalie's volleyball game, wearing my "Nat-Attack!" shirt which I had just made from an old white t-shirt and some markers. I had thought about it all day, and was so excited to get into that gymnasium to show my love and support for her. When her name was called during the line-up, my hollering began.

For the next hour, I was center stage in a crowd full of quiet onlookers. Natty, sitting the bench not playing? "PUT IN NUMBER 32!" Natty coming into the game? "OH BOY, HERE COMES SOME POINTS!" Natty miss a ball? "OH, YOU'RE LUCKY SHE DIDN'T KILL THAT ONE!" Oh, and you don't even want to know my reaction when one of her serves got us a point. Mass hysteria comes to mind.

Then I noticed all the stares. But two different types. The home team visitors were pumped. The coach's daughter turned around and asked if I could come to every game! Natty told me afterwards that all her team-mates love when I come because I pump them up! But the visiting crowd? A much different story. I was a nuisance. I was a problem. I was overly excited and excessively emotional. At one point, the coach for the other team actually came into the stands to ask if I could tone it down! Do you think this quieted me? It actually made me step up the game even more. I knew I was doing my job, and accomplishing what I had come to do.

I love my niece with all my heart. If I love my heavenly father as much, shouldn't I be as proud to be part of his team, and cheer on my brothers and sisters? I finally am. For the first time, as I stand in the bleachers and whoop and holler for my God, I feel the overwhelming encouragement coming from the rest of my team, and smile when I see the anxious faces of the enemy. I'm getting in their head. I'm making them uneasy. They hate to see me walk into the gym. When people criticize my Facebook posts, do I ease up? Nope, I'm posting more. When they tell me this is a fad that will soon fade like every other time, do I give in? Not a chance, I yell louder. And when the very coach of the enemy tries to quiet me, do I shake in my boots? I welcome the challenge to beat it.

So, did my cheering and pride for my niece help her to win every point? Nope. She actually lost more than she gained. But, did it encourage her to know that even in her failures, that there was someone in the crowd that loved her even in the difficult times? Absolutely. You will have your struggles, but remember that in your praise, you make the enemy nervous. I'm cheering you on, Punkin. And next time, when I happen to be facing MY battle, I except to see you in the stands, cheering for me.

"So speak encouraging words to one another. Build up hope so you'll all be together in this, no one left out, no one left behind." 1 Thessalonians 5:11

April 23, 2015

We had an excellent service Sunday at church. I find myself sitting in the audience and yearning to be on stage: singing again, preaching again, volunteering again. I never feel more close to God than when I'm ministering. I miss it terribly, but know that this is a growing season in my life. I must learn first to be a good Christian before I can challenge others to do the same.

I remember my Grandma Koogler very well. One of the greatest things was getting to eat the fruit that she canned. I wonder if you even know what canning is. We all had those grandmothers that were enamored with canning! I remember one such time sitting in her kitchen while she cut up some peaches, preparing them for their long life on the shelf in the basement. I wanted one right then! As she began to add all the spices and secret ingredients to the jar, my desperation grew even more. But she explained that it just wasn't their time yet. "Gavin, if you eat one right now, you'll only taste peach. You'll be missing out on everything else!" They needed to sit in all the juice for a while to really soak up all that heavenly goodness.

We are so quick to do the same with our Christian walk, and you must be aware of this in your own journey. We desperately want to be used by God right now. As soon as we begin our journey with him, we want to take on the world! But we're just not ready yet. In my prayer time this morning, I felt myself simply "soaking" him up. And that is basically the entire point of our prayer time with him. Once again, I'm reminded that none of this is about me. It's all about him.

Someday, when God see's I'm ready, he will finally allow someone to open my jar and bite into my ministry that he's been preparing for the perfect season. And then, when that time comes, they won't taste me, they'll be filled with all the greatness of what I had been soaking in. Even though at times I feel like I've sat on the shelf for way too long, that the dust that's accumulating on my lid is getting way too thick for my liking, what's going on inside the jar is what really matters. You see, I'm just a Walmart peach, but God wants me to be a Paula Dean peach cobbler. You must learn to be perfectly happy during the "shelf" times of your life, soaking him in.

"To you who are parents, I say, show love to your children. You know you love them, but make certain they know it as well. They are so precious. Let them know. Call upon our Heavenly Father for help as you care for their needs each day and as you deal with the challenges which inevitably come with parenthood. You need more than your own wisdom in rearing them."
—Thomas S. Monson

April 27, 2015

You are changing in everything as quickly as we are changing your diaper. My saving grace has finally arrived in the form of you being able to recognize objects and accept them into your baby world…well actually into your baby mouth, as that's where any new object immediately ends up. If you're crying, all I have to do is introduce a toy.

"Whaa, whaa, whaa!! I'm bored! My belly hur-… Whoa, wait just a minute. What's that there? Keys, you say? Hmm, yes those *are* interesting, in fact. Well, I was just getting ready to tell you about my stomach pains, but now for some reason, the pains have dissipated, and I would very much like to see how those colorful keys taste. If you could just mash those into my palm, I will instinctively grasp my fingers around them, and… yep, they're delicious. Why, thank you Dad, these are most delightful. I shall suck on these for the next couple seconds, until the exact moment you sit down on the couch then I shall drop them onto my chest and be unable to grasp them again without your assistance. I will repeat this series of events until I deem the keys have lost my due pleasure, and a new shiny object will need to be introduced."

I have never understood the need for baby's to taste every single object that is placed in front of them. Is it on the same lines as why dogs sniff each other's butts? Is there some sort of chemical reaction that takes place on your tongue to let you know if a certain toy is friendly or not? I don't mind this…yet. Everything you're around has been properly sanitized up to OSHA standards by your mother. I'm just worried about the near future when you become mobile. I've heard horror stories from fellow fathers of turning around to see their kid sucking the life out of an innocent spider they've came across.

The main thing that I don't enjoy now is the enormous and inhuman saliva production that has recently come about as a result. Your top half is constantly moist with a ring of wetness around your neck extending halfway down your torso. I'm shocked you're not severely dehydrated, and half expect your skin to be shriveled like a prune when I undress you.

I'm now required to feed you one baby food a day, according to the daily task list your mom leaves for me before she goes to work. I hate it. The whole process always ends up taking me half the afternoon. You're currently eating green beans and squash. I tried the green beans myself yesterday, and I have to say, not as bad as I had imagined. It tasted like real green beans, just green beans that had already been chewed up and partially digested for my convenience. The squash made me gag, as it did you as well. It was cold from being in the refrigerator so I ran it under some hot water for a few seconds; it immediately turned to water-like consistency. Live and learn.

The worst part about the food feeding is that I make a mess to the height of needing a Stanly Steamer crew on stand-by outside. It's a one ounce jar of baby food, but looks as if Jesus multiplied it for the 5,000 by the time I'm done. I'm ever amazed at the distance such a small mouth can spit food. I need to start prepping the room as if I'm getting ready to paint prior to the feedings; covering all exposed areas with drop cloths and tape. Plus, it doesn't help that you feel the need to suck your thumb between every blessed bite. Now, you have squash on both arms up to the elbows, which then ends up coating your entire upper body. And since your arms never stop flailing about, it's slung as far as the east is from the west. I should have saved us both the time and stuck a piece of dynamite in the jar and lit it. The part that kills me is the fact that you probably only ingested a total of a half teaspoon by the end of the fiasco.

After ground zero is finally cleaned up (half by me and the other half by the dog), you require a bath. The bath routine has frightened me ever since I read those parenting books before you were born. A baby can drown in as little as one-thousandths of an inch of water. You can drown a baby by placing it on a damp washcloth. Babies can drown if you even *think* about water. Next time you're outside mowing and think, "Man, I could use some iced tea right now" you just drowned your baby.

I would have also never guessed that washing a miniature human would be such a challenge. First of all, I've been taught by your mother that there's about a 2 degree water temperature level that is acceptable. I spend 45 minutes kneeling in the bathroom adjusting the hot and cold levels to finally get the perfect temp; usually just in time for the hot water to run out. After this, I have to deal with the water level in your baby tub--not enough and too much of your body is exposed, causing you to succumb to inevitable hypothermia. Too much water and I have to run to the store for a snorkel and an antibiotic for your double ear infection.

Next is the amount of soap. There is a miniscule difference between scrubbing your body with straight water and it looking like I dumped a gallon of Dawn dish soap in the Craig's fountain downtown. And let me be the first to say that "No Tears" shampoo is a scam- I put some in my eyes last week to test it and my eyeballs felt like I had scrubbed them with a wire brush. There's apparently an order you're supposed to go by when washing baby parts. Your mom told them to me a long time ago, but quickly forgot them before you were even dry.

I've never figured out an easy way of adequately washing you in this stupid tub. First off, you're completely squished up in the contraption, which means twice the amount of rolls to deal with. Then, I've yet to find a way to wash your back and butt without putting you face down in the water, which is something I'm trying to steer away from. Attempting to get your arms and legs still long enough to wash between your fingers and toes has become a task equal to finding the fountain of youth. Plus, since you're covered in an excessive amount of soap it's like trying to hold onto an eel covered in butter.

Finally, the post-bath ritual is so intense, I've written up a check off list to follow. First, head to toe lotion that must be properly warmed up by vigorously rubbing my hands together prior to application. (I always feel like Mr. Miyagi getting ready to heal an injured Karate Kid at this part.) Then the diaper is applied to prevent carpet staining. The ears have to be cleaned with a special fat-ended cue tip so I don't end up rupturing an ear drum, then oil rubbed into the hair. Your mom has instructed me in the correct way to brush the 7 hairs on your head so that maximum softness is obtained. Then, we must lie on the floor in just your skivvies for what seems like 6 years to give you "naked time". Last time I attempted to have "naked time" in the house, you were formed so I've put that off for a while or at least until you're potty trained.

> "I have found the very best way to advise your children is to find out what they want to do and advise them to do it."
> —President Harry Truman

April 30, 2015

You're 6 months old! It's hard to believe that you are growing so fast. The one constant that I hear from everyone close to me, is to enjoy every single minute as it goes by so quickly. This has already proven so very true, as it seems like we just got home from the hospital with you yesterday.

As I think back on the last 6 months, I realize that I will turn around and be walking you down the aisle. I have so many dreams for you, and hope you have many of your own. I daydream about what you'll become, and the many things you'll accomplish. Your mommy is constantly looking at you and saying, "You're going to be famous someday, I just know it." Yes, maybe you will, and then maybe you won't. "Famous" is a very subjective word, and could mean something completely different between two separate people. Whether or not you're famous does not matter to me, I simply ask that you give it everything you've got.

GROWING SO FAST

There's a story of a high school student that tried out for track. He decided that it was his goal to beat the best record in his school's history of 10 feet. He practiced every day for months. He fell constantly, and knocked the bar off incessantly, but he continued to practice, because his goal was clear. Finally, he did it. He hit 10 feet and 1 inch. He reached his dream and met his goal! Now, if this had been me, I would have taken the pole, bronzed it, and placed it over my mantle! But, he wasn't satisfied. He started working on 10 feet 2 inches. Then 10 feet 6 inches. Then 11 feet, 13 feet, 15 feet, until he finally won the world record at that time of 16 feet 3 inches.

My point in this story is this: he had 16 feet 3 inches in him the entire time. When he was just starting, that potential was already there to obtain greatness, and he never settled for less. You may one day accomplish great things, but then press yourself further. Challenge yourself daily to raise your bar. You see, greatness is something few people ever think about, so it's something few people will ever obtain. Never become satisfied with what you're doing, and never become content with where you are. You were destined for greatness.

> "Listen to the mustn'ts, child. Listen to the don'ts.
> Listen to the shouldn'ts, the impossibles, the won'ts.
> Listen to the never haves, then listen close to me...
> Anything can happen, child. Anything can be."
> —Shel Silverstein

PART 9

MY MAY FLOWER

May 2, 2015

I was running errands today, and my car broke down. I had a million things to get accomplished on my one day off this week, and then this happens. I was furious. I got it to the side of the road, and lost it. I was screaming, cursing, kicking the car, and throwing a temper tantrum that would have rivaled any you've ever thrown. I called a tow truck and had it hauled over to the local garage to get it diagnosed and fixed. The mechanic finally came out with the verdict: I had run out of gas. I wanted to die. I wanted to crawl under a rock and disappear forever. But I learned a lesson today, and it's one I will pass on to you.

You will face circumstances that will steal your joy and ruin your day. I was having a great day, but I lost it immediately due to a situation that was easily fixable and much smaller than I had realized. Life has a way of magnetizing problems. There should be a side note to every situation in life that states, "Objects in mirror are larger than they appear." You must realize that our lives consist of 10 percent of what happens to us and 90% of how we respond to it. I let the small 10% problem of running out of gas ruin the remaining 90% of my day. I failed by letting by problem affect by attitude. What negative influence did I convey to everyone that had the misfortune of encountering me today? Failure will change you. It's up to you whether you allow that failure to make you bitter or better. Choose more wisely than your father did today.

> *"The storm starts, when the drops start dropping. When the drops stop dropping then the storm starts stopping."*
> —Dr. Seuss

May 4, 2015

It's the beginning of another baseball season, and daddy is pumped! Our beautiful Cardinals have started the year better than any other start in their history, currently sitting at 18 and 6. I've attempted to watch the games with you, but you're sadly still unimpressed. Your time will come when you're as big a fan of the game as I am. If by some terrible chance you end up a Cubs fan, don't be mad that I cut all ties and send you away to be raised in the jungle by monkeys.

I love the beginning of the season. Everyone is sure that their team will be champions and win the World Series. Even the players all have a feeling of excitement, knowing the past years successes or failures have all been wiped away, and everyone has a clean slate. Every team has an equal chance to the crown. But at the end of the year, only one team wins.

This is why we play the game, because the game determines who's better. It's the same way in our lives, Punkin. We talk about our faith, about our strengths, our relationships. We get up from the alter refreshed, and ready to start a new season, forgetting about last year's failures. But for some reason, after one loss we end up throwing in the towel and quitting game. The Cardinals won the World Series in 2006 with a record of 83 wins and 78 losses. They were champions in a year where they won a mere 5 more games than they lost. Don't be dismayed by the losses or the opponents. They will beat you sometimes, but remember that it's our enemies and battles that determine the victor.

Why do we know about David? Because of Goliath. Why do we know about Daniel? Because of the lion's den. What do you think about when I say Noah? The flood, of course. What comes to mind when you hear about Shadrach, Meshach, and Abednego? The fiery furnace. And what made Jesus more than just a prophet? The cross that he died on. We are known by the enemies we defeat and by the battles we win. Don't throw away a potentially championship life after a heartbreaking defeat. That defeat could possibly turn into an amazing crown.

> *"I have heard there are troubles of more than one kind. Some come from ahead and some come from behind. But I've bought a big bat. I'm all ready, you see. Now my troubles are going to have troubles with me!"*
> —Dr. Seuss

May 11, 2015

I've known fear in my life. I've been held up at gunpoint in Los Angeles. I've missed a head-on collision with a semi by inches. Your Papaw had a massive heart attack and they had to shock him back to life, your Mema had a stroke and was rushed into emergency brain surgery. Lord knows I've had my share of fear, but nothing has prepared me for the constant fear that I'll end up accidentally killing you or messing up your life forever.

There is not a minute that goes by when my stupid brain isn't working overtime with all the endless horrible possibilities that could make me an accidental murderer or terrible father. If by some miracle from Heaven above that you've survived long enough to actually be reading this, then God has definitely interceded on my behalf and sent about a zillion armed angels to surround you while you're in my care.

What if while playing your favorite game of me tossing you up in the air and catching you, I don't realize I'm standing under a ceiling fan, and you're flung across the room into the actual lion's den I'd installed to teach you about Daniel?

What if while cleaning your poopy diaper, I accidentally wipe back to front instead of the correct front to back technique, and you end up with the Black Plague and forced to yell "UNCLEAN" over and over whenever you're in public?

What if while reading the Bernstein Bear's books to you, you get the idea that all bears are friendly moral-driven families and move out to go live with them, only to accidentally come across the *Pearenstein Bear's*, who end up swallowing you whole?

What if I accidentally forget to warm up the lotion in my hands prior to applying it to your fragile baby skin, you end up with severe hypothermia, and I have to keep you in a complete frozen state until there's a cure in the future and I can finally thaw you out?

What if while shopping at Walmart, I'm distracted by the new Plug-In scent "Pepperoni Pizza", and I accidentally tip over the stroller, tossing you down the laundry soap aisle only to be run over by an old lady in a motorized cart?

What if while paying the bills, I accidentally place a stamp on your head instead of the envelope then you end up being raised by the disgruntled electric company employees?

What if I accidentally buy the 1000 watt light bulbs instead of the 100 watt, and end up frying your retina's during your early morning diaper change?

What if I accidentally mix up the puppy's heartworm medicine with your acid reflux medicine, then you grow up being repulsed by fishing for some unknown reason, and the dog is unable to throw up the grass she just ate?

What if I take way too many pictures of you and you end up hating the paparazzi even before your 5th birthday, so much so that you turn down the leading role as Liam Neeson's granddaughter in the new summer Blockbuster, "Taken 14"?

What if I inadvertently choose "plastic" when the grocery store cashier asks, "Paper or plastic?", and then she thinks I'm a horrible father for succumbing you to a possible choking hazard?

What I end up using the Diaper Genie too long, and you grow up thinking your poop actually *doesn't* stink, only to be humiliated on the first day of school in the little girl's room?

What if I wake up you up after stepping on your toy piano while trying to put money under your pillow for your lost tooth, then I have to spend the rest of my life pretending I actually *am* the real tooth fairy?

What if while selling my old tennis racket on eBay, I accidentally upload a picture of you from my computer instead, and then I'll have to ship you to the buyer in Benghazi because I don't want him to leave me any negative feedback?

What if while at the stadium watching the Cardinals play, I catch a homerun from the visiting team, and accidentally throw you back onto the field instead of the ball?

What if on your first day of school, I put you on the Greyhound bus instead of the school bus, and you end up in East St. Louis having to sell your plasma for crayons?

What if I accidentally switch your Flintstone's vitamins with my Men's Daily Ultra vitamin and you end up with way too much iron, so much that you become magnetic and all the silverware starts flying toward you while I'm doing the dishes?

MY MAY FLOWER

What if I lose your pacifier, and tell the old lady next door that has a crush on me that my baby really needs a Nummy, but she thinks I say, "My baby really needs a mommy", and she thinks I got a divorce and ends up kidnapping me and you have to grow up without a father?

What if I'm playing with you on the beach and fall asleep, and then the tide comes in and washes you out to sea?

What if I dress you up as a mouse on Halloween and we're taking pictures in the front yard, but then a hawk swoops down and snatches you up with his razor talons to take to his family of baby hawks for dinner?

What if I make you laugh too much while you're a baby that you don't learn any other emotions and you end up laughing during a funeral and the dead guy's wife starts a fight with you and you knock over the casket that gets you banned from all funeral homes in the state so you have to have my funeral in the Walmart parking lot?

What if I forget your coat and you get hypothermia, or your sunscreen and you get skin cancer, or your toys and you get bored to death, or your formula and you starve? What if I let you go out with wet hair and you get pneumonia, or let you jump on the bed and break a femur, or let you shake your present and end up killing the puppy inside?

I know from talking to other dads whose children have long since left home and started other lives of their own, that this feeling of fear never actually leaves them. As soon as I get you past the fears of falling during your toddler years will be just in time for me to begin fearing that you'll be bullied at school. And as soon as I get you past the fears of school will be just in time for me to begin fearing that some guy will break your heart. I'll be a nervous wreck every time you drive, and every time you leave home. I guess that's just our lot as dads. I'm scared to death, but like every rollercoaster I've ever been on, the thrill of the ride is always worth the fear that precedes it.

GAVIN McDONALD

> *"No matter how calmly you try to referee, parenting will eventually produce bizarre behavior, and I'm not talking about the kids. Their behavior is always normal."*
> —Bill Cosby

May 14, 2015

I've had a sad day. You will inevitably have the same. You really can't explain why, but for whatever reason, you're down. The world around you seems gray, people's voices sound like you're hearing them from under water, and nothing can hold your interest. You roam through your house for no real reason, but to try to get your mind anywhere but in the fog it's settled in. That's been my day. I'm just plain sad.

But guess what, even in the deepest trench of despair that we may find ourselves in, He has never changed. He's not calling us to fight those tall walls, and try to escape. He's not running to your aide with a ladder. He's calling us to understand that even in times of gut-wrecking sadness; he's still the same God.

Remember the blindfolded lady of justice you can find on money and on top of judicial buildings? The weight on one side would determine how much price you'd have to pay on the other to balance the scale. So we begin to pile up the burdens onto one side. The lies you've been told. The promises broken. The family members lost. The people that's ignored you. The loneliness. The fear. The bad breaks, bad health, bad days. Stack them as high as we can, and watch that side plummet.

Now I can imagine God's response. Does he remove them? Does he begin to take away our burdens, our sadness, our lost hope? No, instead of taking them, he simply offsets them. He places the weight of his love on the other side. He begins to throw on Endless Joy. He starts to stack up Measureless Peace. He finishes it off with an Eternity with Him. The scale now is tipping in your favor.

The heaviness of life can at times seem insurmountable, unless we allow our Father to offset our sadness. If we simply allowed God to take every burden, all we'd be left with is an empty scale. An empty life. So, as you sit there reading tonight, I don't ask him to take your sadness. Simply allow any tears that ever stream down your face, to simply fall onto the scale. Sit back and let the excitement fill you as you see what God will use to offset each and every one.

> *"Parents can only give good advice or put them on the right paths, but the final forming of a person's character lies in their own hands."*
> —Anne Frank

May 20, 2015

Almost everyone I know has joined Facebook. And almost everyone I know has also at one point or another has considered giving it up. We've all been there. "I'm done. I'm deleting the account! Okay, well maybe I'll just deactivate it for now, just in case I decide to come back later!" You want to know the reason so many of us want to give it up? It makes us miserable. We log on every single day, look through the pictures and status updates our "friends" post, and come to the conclusion that everyone you know is happier and more successful than we are. We look at other people and feel miserable in comparison.

Hmm, what a crazy phenomenon. It's beginning to look very clear to me that Facebook is exposing something, some nasty little corner of our human heart. Facebook is all about making life seem joyful. We "like" another's happy status updates, not the sad ones; we post photos of our parties, not our funerals; we use it to celebrate births and marriages and new relationships, not to mourn deaths or remember those painful recent break-ups. Facebook is *supposed* to me a happy place for happy people. But it has not worked out so well. We all think everyone else is happy, but we don't feel the joy.

And it goes both ways! When we show ourselves off through social media, we do so on our own terms. We constantly present ourselves in the way we want to be perceived, continually stretching and exaggerating our lives, trying desperately to keep up. We come to the point of actually resenting another person for being happy, thinking: "He has an amazing life and I don't!" Or we resent him for being falsely happy: "Oh, I know him and I know that his life isn't all that!"

One way or another, we all end up feeling miserable. I found a quote online this morning from Libby Copeland about happiness: "If we only wanted to be happy it would be easy; but we want to be happier than other people, which is almost always difficult." Listen to this statement: We do not want to be happy – we want to be happier. It becomes a competition, and place of comparison. But listen… we can never be happier because we constantly drag ourselves down by believing that we are the only ones who are miserable.

What a sad lot we are! What a ridiculous, jealous, envious group!

Facebook now has made me believe, more than ever, in the true value of taking my family to church every week, in the value of true, deep fellowship, and genuine community. When you don't measure your life or happiness by Facebook, but by the real life and real world, well, that is where people see you for who you really are. And they love you on that basis. In fact, they love you MORE on that basis!

The ultimate fact is, we want to love real people and we want to be loved by real people. Facebook is fiction. Our local church is fact – the most real community we can experience this side of eternity. So, think back on the countless times I've dragged you out of bed on Sunday mornings, and realize it was not simply to fulfill the "Christian" obligations. It was to instill deep within you the true meaning of a loving family that meets beyond the four walls of our house.

> *"So let's do it—full of belief, confident that we're presentable inside and out. Let's keep a firm grip on the promises that keep us going. He always keeps his word. Let's see how inventive we can be in encouraging love and helping out, not avoiding worshiping together as some do but spurring each other on."*
> —Hebrews 10:22-25

May 23, 2015

Today, we went to a college graduation party for one of mommy's cousins. I walked into a house full of people and the usual chaos of "Invasion of the Baby Snatchers" commenced. There were times while I was eating and talking to random people that I would have to scan the crowd in an attempt to find you amongst the women passing you around like a platter of hors d'oeuvres. I would be lying if I said I got tired of saying "Thank you" to every person that tells me how beautiful you are. I sat back with a belly full of lunchmeat and a chest full of pride to take in for the millionth time what I had created. I've never been happier to show something off to any random person who happened to pass into my vicinity.

I'll never forget my first trophy. Well, I say "first" as if there were a plethora of awards to follow. Sadly, there were not. Now, if they had happened to give away trophies for "Most Talkative" or "Most Likely to Be Strapped to His Desk by His Teacher", I would have had to convert the garage to a trophy museum. I'm actually glad they didn't, because that's way too much to dust. I was in the third grade when I won this fantastic and glorious trophy for my astonishing science fair skills. Okay, so it was what they refer to as a "participation" award, but try explaining that to an 8 year old. As I was riding the school bus home, clinging tight to my weird gold-colored man holding a torch on a piece of fake granite, I tried to imagine the excitement my parents would experience when they laid eyes on this gem.

For the next two weeks, my little gold man went everywhere with me. "Excuse me pastor, could you maybe mention this little tidbit in your sermon? Thanks." "Yes, the Happy Meal, please. Nothing for this little man though. This is just a trophy. A trophy I won…because I'm awesome. Would you like me to tell you more?" "For Show and Tell this week, I was sure you all wanted to gaze upon this beauty for the third week in a row. Once again, please don your appropriate sterile gloves prior to handling the merchandise." I wanted everyone to know that I had accomplished something great, and I have the proof of that greatness right here in my hands.

You have become my trophy. There are no cashiers, bankers, waitresses, postmen, patients, or random passerby that are safe from my overflowing excitement. Whenever I get into a crowd of people, I'm tempted to jump onto a table and hold you up like Simba in the Lion King to make sure all have a great view. I did this. I created you and nothing could make me more proud than to be able to look at the faces in the crowd and say, "Yep. She's mine. I'm her daddy."

Go with me for just a moment, and put yourself in God's shoes. Imagine him following your every move, and making sure everyone can see you. Watch him as he struts down the streets of gold, with his head high and chest out, holding a trophy in his arms with your name engraved in the granite. "Yep, Peter, this is it. My most prized possession. Do you have any idea what I had to go through to get this?" "No, I'm sorry, you can't hold it. I'm holding on to this one for dear life! I have to protect this baby!" "Hey, Gabriel, do me a favor and clear those galaxies off the mantle, please. I know just the spot for this so everyone can admire my greatest accomplishment."

The level of joy that I feel every time I look at you could never come close to the feelings God has. I've been showing you off with overwhelming pride every day for 7 months, but God has been bragging about you before anything ever was. I get to spend the short amount of time I have on this Earth showing you off as my greatest trophy, but God gets to spend all of eternity showing you of as his. I'll be there with you someday, laughing as we watch God jump up on the dinner table for the billionth time, hold you up for all of Heaven to see, and hear him say, "Yep. She's mine. I'm her daddy."

> "The best words of wisdom that a parent can say to their child is "I Am proud of you"."
> —Unarine Ramaru

May 26, 2015

Today, you celebrated your first Memorial Day. We did the usual things you're supposed to do on this holiday, like barbequing with family, enjoying the nice spring weather, and taking a drive through the cemetery to remember those we've lost. It was the first time I was able to introduce you to your Great Grandma and Grandpa McDonald in the

Cedar Grove Cemetery in Salem. I never had the pleasure of meeting my Grandpa, as he died before I was born, but you would have loved your Great Grandma Mac. She loved to bless others by cooking. That was her gift, and that's what she'll always be known for.

During the drive through the cemetery, I began to think about my own life and about yours. What will we be known for? What will we pass down to our children and grandchildren? Sadly, there will come a day that you will visit me and your children will visit you on Memorial Day. What will spring to their mind first? What stories will they tell their children and what legacy will they remember?

There were once two miners that packed up their families and traveled out to California during the Great Gold Rush of 1849. They worked tirelessly for years, sunrise to sunset, praying and hoping to get lucky. They went home every night with nothing in their hands but calluses and blisters. But then one day it finally happened. They struck pay dirt. They looked down to see shimmering gold peeking through the cracks of rock below them. As they were admiring the sight, the cave started to shake around them, as a mighty earthquake began to shake the town. As rocks crumbled around them, they quickly made their way to the caves entrance, but a huge rock broke free from the ceiling and trapped one of the miners when it landed on his leg. His friend tried desperately to free the man, but quickly realized that it was useless. The rock wouldn't budge.

The trapped miner, accepting his fate, yelled to his friend to get out while he could and save himself. The friend, heartbroken, pleaded and begged for him to try harder. He yelled, "No! You can't give up! What would I tell your wife? What am I to tell your family and friends?!" The trapped miner pulled his friend close, and spoke his last words to him: "Just tell them that I died rich."

The graveyard is the richest place in the entire world. While looking around at the countless gravestones that filled the cemetery, I wonder how many died rich. I'm not talking about rich in money or resources.

I'm talking about the one that went there with the song that he wrote still in his heart, or that story still in their mind, or that vision still in their spirit. They went to their grave rich in the things God had given them, but failed to share it with the world.

Baby, you must live this life for something that will echo in eternity. We are given one chance at this. We don't get a do-over, a mulligan, or a second chance. You're given one. Make this one shot count. My hope is that you leave this life completely empty handed, having left everything that was in your heart and soul for the world to enjoy when you're gone. That's the dream for my life too. Someday, when your children are visiting you during the yearly Memorial Day routine, I pray they stand there for a minute and feel the weight of the legacy you've left for them.

> *"If you would not be forgotten as soon as you are dead, either write something worth reading or do something worth writing."*
> —Benjamin Franklin

PART 10

MY SUMMERTIME SWEETIE

June 2, 2015

Your mother sent me on a baby supply errand today. Over the last few months, this has always proven to be a poor decision. You'd think that after multiple innocent mistakes on my part, that she would have learned her lesson, and decided that it's easier to simply do it herself, but she's sticking with me for some reason. On one of my first trips, I was asked to get "butt paste", which the name itself causes extreme confusion for me. Instead, I ended up bringing home some sort of plaster set that you put your hands and feet in for a weird keepsake. On another similar occasion, I was instructed to get some "burp cloths" and apparently bought a 20 pack of washcloths and 10 pack of cloth diapers.

Needless to say, whenever she comes to me with a baby shopping list, I begin to sweat profusely and throw myself into a mini panic attack. My life's goal during your babyhood, was to attempt to not come across as a complete moron, and so far, I've managed to stay teetering right on the edge the majority of the time. So, when mommy gave me a new list today, I immediately began to pray for wisdom and guidance during my quest.

I've come to the conclusion that the baby department is no place for the dad that's teetering anywhere *near* the edge of fatherhood stupidity, and that the majority of the department has been created by mothers determined to solidify the fact on who's the brighter and most capable in raising a child between the two parental units. Whenever I find myself in the black-hole that is the baby department, I might as well be in a huge Grimace costume from McDonald's, riding a unicycle and juggling 12 live kittens; this is how much attention I draw to myself.

I always catch myself squinting at an object, like I'm staring straight into a solar eclipse, for way longer than any object needs to be examined- and then see the females staring me down in my peripherals, waiting to pounce on the opportunity to help this poor, ignorant male that's accidentally wandered into their domain. This doesn't happen anywhere else in the store. I've never found myself in the chip aisle, trying to decide between Doritos and Pringles, when another random shopper see's my dilemma and runs to my aid saying, "Aww, do you need some help, honey?"

I cannot simply go to the store to buy you a shirt. While browsing through the options, I'm faced with a whole new clothing vocabulary: onesie, romper, sleeper, swaddles, jumpers, sacks, slippers, bamboozlers, cartinkers. I half expected to see the Dr. Seuss logo on the tag. I don't go into the men's section and ask, "Yes, where are your Relaxers? All out? Well, then, how about some TV Watchers or Grass Mowers?" Then, I inevitably end up having to do algebra in my head, trying desperately to remember how many "months" you are. At one point, I'm pretty sure I accidentally went too far into the math, found myself dividing by pi, and somehow ended up bring you home a frozen turkey by accident.

> *"The father of a daughter is nothing but a high-class hostage. A father turns a stony face to his sons, berates them, shakes his antlers, paws the ground, snorts, runs them off into the underbrush, but when his daughter puts her arm over his shoulder and says, "Daddy, I need to ask you something," he is a pat of butter in a hot frying pan."*
> —Garrison Keillor

June 9, 2015

Have you felt like you're stuck in a wilderness? In a long, cold, lonely winter that you feel will never end? Your calendar is stuck in February, and it seems as if you've forgotten the smell of spring. We have all found ourselves in a wilderness, thinking that we have all the answers to find a way out.

Many years ago, when your daddy was a little boy, we were on one of our yearly Florida family vacation and came across a large tourist trap. Literally. A giant maze. Row after row of 8 foot wooden walls, leading to one dead end after another. Successfully navigate the labyrinth, and you can climb a large tower in the center. If you were to look at our family pictures of the trip, you'd see four of our five family members standing in the top of the tower. Hmmm, I wonder who's still on the ground? Guess who? I couldn't for the life of me figure out which way to go. Ah, but then I heard a voice from above. "Hey, Gav!" I looked up to see my Dad, peering at me from the tower. "You're going the wrong way. Back up and turn right!"

Do you think I trusted him? I didn't have to. I could have trusted my own instincts, consulted other confused tourists, sat and cried and wondered why God would let this happen to me. But do you know what I did? I listened. His vantage point was better than mine. He was above the maze. He could see what I couldn't.

Don't you think we should do the same with God? In Job, the Bible says, "God is higher than the Heavens!" Can he not see what we can't? Does he not want to get us out and bring us home? We don't always understand why we have to go through some of the wildernesses that crush our spirit, but before you throw in the towel and quit, try looking up. God may just be whispering the direction to go.

> *"Fix these words of mine into your mind and being, and tie them as a reminder on your hands and let them be symbols on your forehead. Teach them to your children and speak of them as you sit in your house, as you walk along the road, as you lie down, and as you get up. Inscribe them on the doorframes of your houses and on your gates."*
> —Deuteronomy 11:18-20

June 13, 2015

Baby brains are funny. Your little mush of gray between your ears still believes that if you can't see it, than it surely must not even exist. I love the fact that I can walk into a room and your face lights up, as if you're thinking, "Hey, for some reason, this figure brings me joy, although I have no idea why!" Then the moment I leave the room, your little mind begins to immediately think, "Umm, I seem to vaguely remember an apparition that took care of this awful smell in my pantaloons… Whelp, guess I have nothing better to do than to cry about this situation until that thing returns."

So, your brain definitely has some major maturing to accomplish, although it *is* making some small steps toward being able to hold a place in normal human interaction. You are now able to find substantial joy in various inanimate objects. I could present you with a used tissue, DVD case, or the electric bill and you're content for a crazy length of time. For some reason, one of your favorites is the smiling sun toy on your Jumparoo. Today, as I was watching you become overwhelmed with happiness from a piece of colorful plastic, I came to the realization that the joy on your face is exactly the same joy I see when you're looking at me. So, I'll be the first to admit that a small tinge of jealousy rose in my chest.

"Oh, you like that sun, do ya? That sun doing a great job of changing your butt?! Oh, whatcha crying for? You hungry? Well, why don't you just have that SUN MAKE YOU A BOTTLE, THEN?!"

Yeah, I'm sorry about that. Don't worry, I eventually did get you a bottle and, yes, I apologized to the smiling sun. He was simply doing the job I hired him to do. I know there will come a day when you really do appreciate all the things I do for you. I just hope at that point the happiness I see on your face isn't the same as the happiness I see when you're staring at your cell phone.

I noticed another first today. I came in from getting the mail and didn't realize that I had accidentally dropped a piece of the newspaper in your grasping vicinity. I went about my chores until I heard an unfamiliar rustling coming from the living room. I came back to find you thoroughly enjoying the sports section. And by thoroughly enjoying, I mean chewing on it like a dollar store steak. I quickly swooped in to take it from you. I realized this was the first time I had to take something from you that you shouldn't have. Did you just go on to one of the other 78 toys I had surrounded you in? Nope, you pouted up and began wailing. For some reason, I thought it necessary to begin explaining to you the reasoning on why it must be confiscated, as if you were going to say, "Oh, Father, I had no idea! I deeply apologize for the actions brought about by my selfish demeanor, and will strive to better my attitude toward similar circumstances in the future."

Well, shockingly, you failed to listen to my fatherly advice, and just continued to wail. So, did I take this opportunity to begin to strengthen your character and succumb you to the many disappoints that this life will serve up? Nope, I quickly gave the newspaper back; although I did exchange the wet and crumpled sports section for the classifieds. So as we both sat there in the floor enjoying the paper, I contemplated giving you a sip of my coffee, just to complete the moment, but didn't want the black smear that was all over your face to get on my new Cardinal's mug.

"A truly rich man is one whose children run into his arms when his hands are empty."
—Unknown

June 18, 2015

I've spent the day in a class for work called ENPC, or Emergency Nursing Pediatric Course. It was, as always, painstakingly boring and torture for your ADHD riddled father, but there was one thing I took away from the lesson. According to Erik Erikson's psychosocial stages of development, the very first stage in life is Trust, and is learned by an infant even before their first birthday. During this stage, the infant is uncertain about the world around them, and they instinctively turn to their caregiver for stability and protection.

I pray that as you've grown, you have come to realize that you can trust me completely, and I would never put you in harm's way. I also know that in my human state, there will sadly come a time that I will fail you and break that trust in some way. But in this, you must remember that Jesus, your ultimate caregiver and Father, will never ever compromise that trust. He will never fail you.

I trust him. Do you realize how hard that actually is to do? Oh, it's easy to say, but to actually trust him with everything? Not so easy. I remember one of your cousin Natty's favorite games ever (and I'm sure soon to be yours as well!) was to stand on the edge of the bed, and jump out into my arms. She couldn't get enough! My arms would be bruised and bleeding by the time she even thought of getting tired of the game! But the first time she jumped was a different story. I tried and tried to tell her how much fun it would be. Told her over and over that she had nothing to worry about. I whispered to her "Natty…trust me." With a heart overflowing with apprehension, she inched closer to the edge of the bed. With eyes full of fear and doubt, she finally let loose, and flailed into my arms. I caught her. I promised that I would, and I did.

Trust is one of the hardest things in life to learn to do. Especially when it involves staring wide-eyed into the unknown. We have no idea what we're facing. The bible speaks of Paul sitting in jail. Not overnight, or for a few months…for years he sat there with nothing to accompany him but his own thoughts. Did he have family there to help him through the tough times? Nope. How about all the things he owned to pass the time? He had nothing. Lots of friends to pray with him? Not a one. A good reason for him being there? No way. Reputation? Health? Sunday morning church to pump him up? No. No. And No. The only thing that got him through was his unrelenting and undying trust.

I have no idea what the next few days, months, or years has in store for you. If you would ask me to explain why God allows you to go through some of the trials that you will face or have faced, I couldn't give you a response. But guess what… we weren't created to understand God;

we were created to love and trust him. You may be in pain in life right now. You may be hurting. But listen to this: God cannot use greatly who has not hurt deeply. Pain is God's megaphone.

Today, you may be looking at your unknown circumstances and future with a heart overflowing with apprehension--just ease closer to the edge. With eyes full of fear and doubt, choose today to let loose, and throw yourself into the arms of a loving God that's simply whispering, "Kinley…trust me." And now after feeling the surge of adrenaline that goes along with trusting God, I guarantee you'll be eagerly crawling back onto the bed to do it again. And again. And again.

> *"Trust in the LORD with all your heart and lean not on your own understanding."*
> —Proverbs 3:5

June 21, 2015

Father's Day. I've said, "Happy Father's Day" to countless dads over the years. I never knew what it would feel like to have it said to me. I've had people wish me Merry Christmas many times, and have received innumerous "Happy Birthday's" over the years. But this one's different. It's a statement specifically directed towards me to acknowledge something I've accomplished. I had nothing to do with my birthday. I had no hand in creating Christmas, New Year's, or Thanksgiving. This holiday was made just for me.

With this being my first year of eligibility, the statement was usually quickly followed by a question: "So how does it feel being a father?" I've never been asked a harder one. If you would ask me how it feels to be a human, I could probably come up with an answer. If you asked how it feels to drive a car, or kiss my wife, or swim in the ocean, I could find the right words to compare with those feelings. Not this. I can't find the words.

As I sat in church this morning, I looked around at all the dads. I was part of them. I was part of this elite group of men and proud to be one of their newest members. But then I remembered that this is a pretty large group! I'm one of billions! I realized *becoming* a father is not the great part, but in all the things we do after. Just as putting on a ring doesn't make me a great husband, getting mommy pregnant doesn't make me a great dad. So, how do I become one of the greats? How do I move up in the rankings and eventually be elected to the "Fatherhood Hall of Fame"?

I've found the answer, and it's shockingly simple. Love you. Love you with such an intensity that my whole life centers around it. The ones that have mastered this simple rule have in turn shown what it truly means to be a great father.

I love you. I love you so much it hurts. I find myself saying it to you over and over as if you have any idea what I'm saying, but it doesn't matter. I want you to know, and I'll tell you every day single day for the rest of my life. I don't want you to ever forget, even after I'm gone. It's painful to be apart from you, even miserable at times. You're all I think about. I'm obsessed, and never been more excited to live my life.

This is what makes a father great. An overwhelming love for someone makes you do everything in your power to protect them, provide for them, and pray for them. A love that says, "Even if you end up not liking me, or possibly even hating me, I will love you anyway. Forever."

MY SUMMERTIME SWEETIE

> *"One of the greatest things about daughters is how they adored you when they were little; how they rushed into your arms with electric delight and demanded that you watch everything they do and listen to everything they say. Those memories will help you through less joyous times when their adoration is replaced by embarrassment or annoyance and they don't want you to see what they are doing or hear what they are saying. And yet, you will adore your daughter every day of her life, hoping to be valued again, but realizing how fortunate you were even if you only get what you already got."*
>
> —Michael Josephson

June 25, 2015

While going through my usual daily tasks in all things babyhood today, I've come to realize that everything is different for a child. I have socks that keep my feet warm, tongue for taste, and ears to hear. I've searched Amazon for an appropriate baby book to buy you so that you may learn what all these objects are actually intended for in everyday society.

You don't use your socks for warmth, but as a fun scavenger hunt for daddy. I can't go to a store without noticing (usually while halfway through the check-out process) that you've managed to lose a sock sometime in the last 45 minutes. I then spend the majority of what's remaining in the afternoon attempting to retrace my steps throughout the supercenter in search of the lost clothing item. By the time I eventually find it in some random aisle I don't even remember visiting, I look down to notice the other one is now missing in action. At this point, I usually just count it as a loss, and head for the baby section to buy more socks.

You don't use your tongue for taste, but as some sort of gatekeeper to prevent any entrance into the mouth. During the 17 hours in attempting to feed you the 2 ounces of green beans, 16 hours and 45 minutes is spent desperately trying to get the spoon past the goalie. I end up having to use the spoon to sort of smash the tongue down into submission in order to get the mush scraped off onto the back of the pallet. I've heard them say the tongue is apparently the strongest muscle in the body, but this is ridiculous. I wouldn't be surprised to look down and see that yours has abs- or at least holding a hockey stick, wearing a goalie mask, and yelling, "Come at me, bro!"

You don't use your ears to hear, but rather as a hidden reservoir for vomit. I didn't understand for months why the Q-Tip would come out brown when your ears were cleaned after the nightly bath, but I finally figured it out. You lay on your back, spit up, and gravity takes over, allowing the nastiness to travel directly into the ear saucers. I imagine your ears saying, "Hey! I'll just store this goodness in here in case I get hungry later! And you know what? If I happen to get bored, I'll just use it to crank up a good ole infection to keep me nice and toasty with the million degree fever it starts!"

You don't use your clothing as its normal skin protector, but as a way to make daddy feel like scum when he manages to constantly harm you with it. It never fails that when trying to pull your sleeves on, halfway through the tunnel, your thumb decides to jump ship and gets all tangled up to the point of me practically breaking it off at the knuckle. For the longest time, I couldn't understand why you hated sleeves so much and began to cry when getting them put on, but now I realize it's because daddy was ripping off one of your body parts in the process. Also, for a man that's put on countless shirts in his life, you would think I'd be able to get one over your face without suffocating the very breath out of your lungs. Even with the extra girth they provide in the head hole for a baby's gigantic melon, it always seems to get trapped, and then I'm struggling to set you free and regain air to your oxygen deprived body. The look on your face when I finally get the head through is one that's always seems to be telling me, "Geez, dad. You trying to murder me? Get it together."

> *"To the world you may be one person; but to one person you may be the world."*
> —Dr. Seuss

June 28, 2015

When we take a simple trip to Salem to see your Mema and Papaw, the diaper bag is full enough that it practically requires wheels to get it to the car. So, you can imagine what it was like preparing for a two day trip to Springfield this week. Halfway through loading the car, I was getting close to having to rent a pull-behind U-Haul. Your mom went completely overboard (shocker). We could have easily went to live on a deserted island, and been adequately stocked until your 8th birthday.

It took me so long to haul everything into the hotel room that it was practically time to turn around and load everything back up by the time I was done. You had four bags, your mom had 2, and daddy could fit everything he needed for a *one night trip* into a Walmart sack. I was expecting a knock on the door at any minute and it would be the FedEx man with your dresser.

This week was another huge first for as you stayed the night with Aunt Teetee. Daddy had to get a procedure on his back done, and since we needed to leave town at 6 in the morning, it was really our only option. Your poor Mommy was a train wreck. Your Aunt came and picked you up the evening before, and watched you ride away for the first time in your life. I was close to throwing up, but needed to stay strong for your Mommy, as she was close to slipping into a coma.

It was a strange night with you not here. I found myself sitting on the couch and coughing into the pillow as I always do when you're asleep to minimize the sound. I kept glancing at the monitor showing the empty crib, and I finally broke down into quiet sobs. I didn't know what to do with myself. I paced the halls, and prayed you'd be safe. I walked outside and then came back in. I was a lost. For the first time, I felt what life would be like with you not in it. Empty and lonely.

I imagine God can sympathize. There are countless times in our life that we walk away from him. We leave him to follow our own dreams and passions, as he sits on his couch agonizing over whether you're safe or not. Wondering if you're happy and being taken care of. I envision him pacing the halls of Heaven; tossing and turning in bed, unable to get you off his mind.

And then imagine his overwhelming joy when you finally decide to come back to him. I can tell you what it was like for me. When we heard you were on your way back home, we sat on the couch, staring out the window, waiting as the minutes felt like hours. When I finally saw Aunt Teetee's car, my stomach turned. My throat clinched up in happiness, and your Mommy ran out to get you. For the rest of the evening, we couldn't let you go.

Remember that God never leaves us, we can only leave him. And when we do, we leave him broken hearted and counting the minutes to see you finally pull back into the driveway. And I promise that for the rest of eternity, he won't let you go.

MY SUMMERTIME SWEETIE

> *"I have no greater joy than to hear that my children are walking in the truth."*
> —John 1:4

June 30, 2015

Well, I let you fall today. You're still perfecting the act of sitting up on your own, so as I was practicing with you today, you took a tumble. These are nothing new, as you fall over constantly, but this time you smacked your head on the end table. Your face scrunched up, and your eyes went wide, and I knew a scream was on its way. As I held you close, and began kissing your boo-boo, I prayed silently that you didn't have an intracranial bleed- oh the mindset of an ER nurse.

Your failure is not final. I know by now you've heard me tell you this countless times before, but it's definitely worth repeating. It's not falling down that makes you a failure, it's staying down. Look at yourself in the mirror and constantly remind yourself who you are. You must get back up.

I was watching Sports Center the other day while they were showing a special on Hall of Famer Barry Sanders. He ran for over 15,000 yards in his career! That's incredible! But you know the most amazing fact? He averaged only 4 yards per carry. This means that every four yards, he was taken down. He was constantly picking himself back up, and trying again. For many of us, we fall down after four yards, and we end up just lying there for four years! Stand up, dust yourself off, and go again. And again. And again.

I'm reminded of one instance where I came crying to *my* mom. I'm pretty sure I was doing something I wasn't supposed to, which was often. I ran into the garage screaming, blood coming from my knees and elbows. My mom tried to calm me down enough to hear what happened. She scoops me up, and does what all good moms do. Now get this: Even though I had disobeyed her. Even though I did what she specifically told me NOT to do, my mom made a decision that my pain was penalty enough. She didn't go get the fly-swatter and give me a spanking while I was bleeding. She could've easily done that, because it's what I rightfully deserved. But she didn't. She began to bandage me up, clean my wounds, dust me off, and wipe my tears. She knew that in the pain of the fall would come an everlasting remembrance to never do that again. It was the pain of the fall that made all the impact that I needed. She would end it with, "Now tell me what we're not going to do again."

I am so happy that while I was trying to learn how to sit up, that every time I failed, my mom didn't scream "Well, look what you did, you bald little loser!" We are all learning how to do this thing we call life. We have all fallen. If you are living and breathing right now, you have failed. And guess what, if you are still living and breathing this time next week, then you will fail again!

On judgment day, the Bible says that a man tugs on Jesus' robe and asks, "Who are all these people in white robes?" And He answers, "These are the ones that have come out of great troubles. I found them in the middle of trouble, and their robes have been washed." See, you don't need washed without falling and getting dirty first. Just because you fall, doesn't mean you can't get back up.

I am so sorry that you fell today. And I'm even sorrier if you have fallen spiritually in your life. I know how it feels to hit the ground. Nothing about it is easy, and it always hurts terribly. But never forget the pain. The pain will keep you from ever wanting to go through it again. Learn from your mistakes, get back up, dust yourself off, and push for another 4 yards. Who knows, someday you might just find yourself in God's Hall of Fame.

MY SUMMERTIME SWEETIE

> *"Children are people, and they should have to reach to learn about things, to understand things, just as adults have to reach if they want to grow in mental stature. Life is composed of lights and shadows, and we would be untruthful, insincere, and saccharine if we tried to pretend there were no shadows. Most things are good, and they are the strongest things; but there are evil things too, and you are not doing a child a favor by trying to shield him from reality. The important thing is to teach a child that good can always triumph over evil."*
>
> —Walt Disney

July 3, 2015

Begin to live your life for a purpose greater than yourself. Do something with your one and only life that will count for eternity. My whole purpose in this life is to take hold of the purpose God has for me. Yes, I'm sure you have tons of dreams, but your sole purpose is not to have those fulfilled! I know God looks at our little insignificant dreams and grins to himself, knowing full well the dreams *He* has handcrafted for you blow yours out of the water.

    I recently have begun to look into investing in some stocks to help pay for your college and wedding. There are countless options to choose from, and it's hard to find the perfect one that will give me the greatest return. Listen to me: the value of your life can be determined by what you invest your life in. Let me explain this to you. If we went to Lowe's tonight and bought a solid steel bar, we would spend a total of about 2 bucks. But say we decided to melt that bar down, and make penny nails. The value of that 2 dollar bar then goes to twenty dollars. But instead of nails, we made sewing needles. The value would then jump to 200 bucks. Let's take it further: we decided to melt down that 2 dollar bar and make fine cutlery, or knives. All of a sudden that value of that bar jumped to over two thousand dollars. But say we didn't make nails, needles, or knives, but instead make Swiss Watch springs. The value of that cheap steel bar has now reached nearly two million dollars.

So, what changed its worth? What made something that was so cheap, suddenly so valuable? What it was invested in. Begin today to start investing your life into what God wants for you. There are many times in this life that you may feel worthless. Have you ever looked at your circumstances and felt like you were a dime a dozen? That you were making no impact on this one life you've been given? Have you ever felt that after you're gone, the only thing that will remain is a tombstone? Just remember that even though everyone around you, including yourself, may see you as nothing more than a cheap steel bar, God sees Swiss Watch springs. Apart from God, you really are nothing, but *with* him, you are everything. Invest your life in God, and watch your value soar.

"My father gave me the greatest gift anyone could give another person, he believed in me."
—Jim Valvano

July 4, 2015

Your first fourth was a success. You were able to don your appropriate red, white, and blue, watch a patriotic parade, eat your first Popsicle, and you never once caught fire from your cousins erratic sparkler waving.

MY SUMMERTIME SWEETIE

Yes, I would call that a tremendous success. I went to BOOMTOWN yesterday to purchase you a few necessary fireworks, but it ended up taking me roughly 2 hours to decipher through all the random names and explanations to be sure not to get any with earth shaking explosions. I intend to keep your eardrums intact…well, until the Cardinals make the playoffs, at least.

I was so confused sorting through the fireworks tent, looking at names like (and *none* of these are made up) *The Punisher, Just Awesome, Saddam Bomb, Warm Greeting, That's Your Problem, Acid Rain, Redneck Ruckus,* and my personal favorite *Larry.* How on God's green earth am I to know if *Larry* is or isn't filled with 20 pounds of eardrum shattering dynamite? I stuck with the safe fountains, snap pops, black snakes, sparklers, and Chicken Laying Eggs. You're welcome, tiny baby ears.

I remember growing up and spending hours in the yard with your Uncle Nathan leading up to the Fourth, setting off thousands of bottle rockets. We couldn't get enough. After a while, the simple "going up in the air and popping" wasn't enough though, and we inevitably began the act of modifying and creating. We would twist all the wicks together in one pack and set them all off at once (they all went off at once roughly 7% of the time). We would find an innocent by standing toy and tape it up with a bazillion rockets in the attempt to send it to orbit (it got off the ground more than a foot roughly 7% of the time). We even had our perfectly safe game of breaking off the stick, lighting the fuse, dropping it between us, and then running like mad men (I ended up with a circular burn on my calf roughly 97% of the time.)

But then something happened. We found bigger and better fireworks. We were introduced to the Roman candle that we could actually *hold* and shoot at each other. We fell in love with M-80's that could blow a small hole in the ground. Then came bigger rockets, huge fountains, 1,000-pack rolls of Black Cats, parachute men that you chased only to end up with eight-degree burns on your palms if you were lucky enough to catch it. The bottle rocket became obsolete.

Tonight, I walked over to the neighbor's house to find their boys setting off bottle rockets. They were having so much fun, running back and forth lighting one rocket at a time, repeating endlessly until a new punk needed prepared. Then I set off one of *mine*. It detonated out of the canister and sailed into the ear, exploding high above us and filling the whole sky with yellow, green, blue, crackles, and whistles. 'MERICA!!! The boys cheered! The parents OOO'd and AAH'd! I had inadvertently ruined their previous fulfillment and content with bottle rockets.

As you become a young woman, you will begin to determine who you will become. What destiny will you decide to create? How many lives will you affect and change? Will you become a church attendee or a church builder? Will you innocently share with people that you're a Christian, or go much deeper and plead with them about the saving love of Christ? Will you simply be a God follower or become a God chaser?

If you live your whole life simply following God, that's perfectly fine, and you will just make the cut into Heaven, but you have no idea the fulfillment and joy you'll receive by going for something greater. Don't live your life as a bottle rocket when you have "*The Star Spangled Banner Mega Missile*" as another option. One more thing on fireworks: You have to light the fuse. It doesn't matter if you're a bottle rocket, a sparkler, or a tremendous fountain cannon that ends up lasting 45 minutes, it's simply a pretty package without the heat source.

I can remember specific times in my life where I've witnessed someone's fuse being lit. The quiet old man in the back pew suddenly jumps up and starts dancing down the aisle. The pastor whose words that God is pouring out of him is instantly overcome to the point of losing the ability to stand. The entire choir that falls to their face from the heaviness of the spirit. The drug addict that is finally free from his addiction after years of slavery telling everyone he meets about the power of freedom in Christ. Before their fuse was lit, all they amounted to was a pretty package.

So decide today to become something extraordinary. Strive to live your life in a way that makes everyone around you gasp with OOO's and AHH's. I can imagine God instructing everyone to step back as he bends down, lights your fuse, and turns around to whisper, "Are you guys ready? Because this is going to be *really* good."

> *"You do not have to make your children into wonderful people. You just have to remind them that they are wonderful people. If you do this consistently from the day they are born, they will believe it easily."*
> —William Martin

July 6, 2015

Every time we go to the doctor, we get a pamphlet with a list of "benchmarks" that you should have mastered at this point in your young life. I hate these with a passion. It never fails that your mother pours over these as requirements you must possess prior to graduating to the next 3 month segment, and inevitably there's always a couple that you're *slightly* behind on. At this point, we go home and mommy goes into boot camp mode for a few days, trying to get you on track with all the other babies on the block.

The most recent list had "crawling" as an expected development for you at this time…shoot. This one has been a hard one to practice. Don't get me wrong, you are able to get to all four corners of the living room, but it's by way of the constant rolls and flips. I've been told all the tricks: put something right out of their reach, put her knees under her, apply mattress springs to her belly.

I'm not sure if you're having a hard time with the concept, or if you're just not that interested. You're definitely making progress though. Seeing as your mother would have to be hospitalized in a mental institution if she missed your first crawl, I'm constantly having to yell through the house to "COME HERE!! COME HERE NOW, SHE'S GONNA DO IT!!" for her to arrive to find you inevitably having flopped happily onto your back once again.

The whole "dangle something they want out of reach" technique has proved worthless. This could actually work if there was one thing you just *really* loved and had to have immediately, but that's simply not the case. You'll look at the rubber set of rings I've placed a foot in front of you, begin to hike that knee up, but then notice that string on the floor next to you is just as interesting. I've attempted to construct a hat with a pole and string that suspends said keys in front of your face, but the keys are too heavy and always end up falling off.

But there *is* a small little improvement this week, as you've learned if you put *both* knees underneath your belly, you can then kind of "hop" forward about half an inch. You remind me of those cheap plastic frogs, that you can press down on the back and they leap forward. It's quite a long process for the little reward that you receive, and you usually give up well before you arrive at the toy. Okay, that's a lie. After about 3 hops, daddy's ADD kicks in and I end up just giving it to you. You're a baby and shouldn't have to work yourself into a sweat for some playtime. Don't tell mommy that practice only lasted a few seconds today.

> *"The attitude that you have as a parent is what your kids will learn from, more than what you tell them. They don't remember what you try to teach them. They remember what you are."*
> —Jim Henson

July 9, 2015

Well we almost met Jesus together today. As I was driving home from the store, I noticed the dark and ominous clouds forming overhead. Then a monsoon hit. You know the worst thing that can happen when driving through a storm? Your wipers going out. Talk about me going into a panic attack driving down the road at 30 mph with you sitting in the back seat, completely unaware of our possible impending doom. My windshield quickly became covered, sight plummeted, and heart rate skyrocketed. I could hardly see where my lights were hitting the road in front of me. Meteorologists call his zero visibility. My hands were tied, my knuckles were white, and I couldn't find myself home.

This winter, during the record snow that hit Boston, Fox News did a special on a terrible snow storm that hit the north in the 1800's. The ones who survived relied simply on markers to show them the way. Two boys set out from school in the storm towards home. The wind laced needles of snow in their eyes. The drifts pulled on their feet. The whiteness covered the roads and trails. Soon they realized they had no idea where to go. Then, just for a moment, they spotted a row of trees. The boys recognized them as the trees their father planted. The trees lined a path from their front porch. If they could move from tree to tree, they would be home.

My windshield wipers went out, and I was only able to make it safely home, because I drove 5 miles an hour and used each passing yellow dash as a guide to keep myself on the road. If you find yourself in a storm today, maybe this is just what you need. The sudden storm that has hit your life has possibly left you blind and disoriented. Do you need a series of markers to guide you home? Make one. Through the years I have found this question a good one to ask in times of crisis. "What do you still have that no one can take?" Granted, the storms can take much, but they can never take all. So, right in the midst of the snowstorm, make your list. I made mine:

What the storm has *not* taken from me: The promise of Heaven, a family who loves me, a God who knows me, and Jesus' word to guide me. Make your list; then, like the boys in the blizzard, let it lead you to a safe place.

"Someday, when the pages of my life end, I know that you will be one of its most beautiful chapters."
—Unknown

July 13, 2015

2:30 in the morning. Look it up in the Guinness Book of World Records, and you'll find it under the heading of "Worst time of day in the history of days and times". There's a reason why the Daylight Savings Time committee chose this hour to completely skip over once a year, and I'm convinced that those unfortunate enough to land themselves in Hell will be stuck in a constant Groundhog Day-ish loop of the 2 to 3 AM timeframe.

Why your body chooses *this* time every night to suddenly become ravishingly starving is a complete mystery. It's as if your brain has placed an evil alarm clock to awaken due to the desperate need of nourishment. This is my punishment. The punishment for what I put my *own* parents through on a daily basis. All my faults are being heaped back upon me in the form of a nocturnal binge-eating baby, and somewhere my parents are reading this - enjoying every single syllable, throwing their heads back in laughter and delight.

The middle-of-the-night feeding is a delicate ecosystem. There are a hundred rules and regulations to meticulously follow; you mess up one single item, and the whole system crashes down upon you. Instead of a quick feed and right back to sleep, it becomes a feed and then happy-baby-party-time-until-sunrise-then-sleep-all-day-thus-ruining-all-routines-for-the-rest-of-babies-and-parents-exsistance.

The first task is making it to your room without fatally injuring yourself. I'm to the point of setting up night-vision camera's to see who's sneaking in my house at night and moving all the furniture. "Hmm, last time I checked there wasn't a chest of drawers in the middle of the HALLWAY!!!"- says my fractured tibia. I inevitably cause significant harm to myself every night, and while rolling on the floor crying, I must remain completely silent. The inability to scream for some reason multiplies all pain by a trillion percent. So it normally takes me around 3 hours to make it to your room, since I'm sweeping the floor slowly with my feet in the darkness 4 inches at a time as if I'm searching for land mines.

The second task is to accomplish all activities while doing so under 3 decibels. I was feeding you one night and Mommy got up to use the restroom. For some unearthly reason, she flushed the toilet. She might as well have been holding a drum line competition in the bathroom. YOU NEVER FLUSH THE TOILET! You swung your head in the direction of the commotion with a look on your face that said, "Hey, was that noise? It must be morning! Father, fetch me my toys and put on a pot of coffee!" Other sound cancelling tactics include the following: opening the door to the microwave before the buzzer sounds on your formula water, sneezing and/or coughing into a pillow, buying WD40 by the case, chloroforming the dog.

Another obstacle is that I'm required to feed you in your room in complete darkness. If there happens to be a *molecule* of light in the room, everything suddenly becomes the most interesting things you've ever seen. "Whoa, whoa, whoa… Dad, do you see what I see?! Is that… is that a WALL?! Do NOT tell me that has always been there… it's…

it's…AMAZING! Ugh, Dad, quit trying to rock me, I'm trying to push myself up to see more of this WALL!!!"

I can see just enough in the darkness to tell if you're looking at me in my peripheral vision – I can NOT make eye contact with you during this fragile time. If I do, you'll smile, then I'll smile, then you'll laugh and it's all over. I might as well get you dressed and take you to the circus at that point. The few minutes this lasts, I stare blankly into the darkness waiting for the sound of you sucking air, my only clue that the bottle is empty. During one extra-boring feeding, I made the ultimate mistake of pulling out my phone to secretly play a little Candy Crush to pass the time- well in the darkness of that tomb it looked as if I'd pulled a semi-truck into the room and blazed the bright lights into your face.

Rocking you back to sleep is also quite the undertaking, as it usually works better on daddy than you. Don't tell mommy, but I'll be the first to admit that there's been multiple occasions that I've jerked myself awake *several* minutes later to you wide eyed and staring at me like, "Wow, Dad, way to play it safe. It's a miracle I'm not face down in the floor."

"He had been searching for it his entire life. He had devoted himself to poetry to find it. Now, in the middle of his life, he found it. It was in the face of the love of his life, his daughter. She who had never blushed before, now blushed. And in that blushing, he knew, was the existence of God. That was the day her father learned what God was. God was pure beauty; God was his daughter's face when she blushed."
—Roman Payne

July 19, 2015

Every person I come across in my life now asks the same exact question: "How is that little girl of yours?" And my response that is now hard-wired into my brain is the same every single time: "Growing like a weed!" I've heard zillions of people say this same thing, and never truly understood it until now, but it's completely true. I understand it even more now, since I rarely have 7 free minutes in the day to mow, and my yard will soon be requiring a hay baler. I attempted to mow the front yard yesterday, but with it being so high, I ended up brutally murdering approximately 17 turtles.

Your teeth are coming in at an alarming speed. It's hard to determine the location and size of aforementioned teeth, due to the fact that when I try to stick my fingers in to feel around, I just end up getting my eyeballs scratched out. Plus the fact that they're now razor sharp, so I'm surprised I have any fingers left at all.

Your love for TV has progressed to a possible unhealthy level. I distinctly remember the conversation between your mommy and me before you were born: "Our baby is NOT going to be a television baby. We are definitely not going to just use that as a babysitter and distraction technique." Oh, how ignorant we were! It allows me just enough of a distraction to satisfy those pesky human needs like using the restroom and consuming food without having to jump up every 6 seconds to save you from possible harm. The one thing that cracks me up though is that your little brain hasn't figured out the most comfortable position for TV watching. I frequently find you in a corner with your back to the room, craning your neck around 180 degrees to stare at the cartoons. I sit on the couch and laugh at you, like dads are supposed to do. When you see me laughing, you usually begin laughing back, I'm sure thinking that I am simply enjoying the show as much as you are.

GAVIN McDONALD

> *"There is a humility of being a father to someone that's so powerful, as if he were only a narrow conduit for another, greater thing. That's how it feels right now, he thinks, kneeling beside her, rinsing her hair: as though his love for his daughter will outstrip the limits of his body. The walls could fall away, even the whole city, and the brightness of that feeling would not wane."*
> —Anthony Doerr

August 6, 2015

It was as if a light switch were flipped in your brain. Your knees accidentally went forward in sync, which caused your body to move in a certain direction. You began to crawl. The look on your face was priceless, and I'm sure "A Whole New World" from Aladdin was playing in your mind. You were off to the races.

It had actually been fairly easy to this point. I could sit you down in a certain place, go do a load of laundry, then come back to you in that same place. Oh, how the tides have turned. I now sit you in a certain place, glance at my watch, then look up to notice you're gone. I expect any minute now, I'll end up finding you uptown crawling 90 mph down Pine Street, but lucky for me you'll undoubtedly leave a nice trail of socks for me to track you down.

The crawling has now opened up all the possibilities this little house has to offer, like crawling into a preheated oven. So, mommy had to order a pallet of baby gates to keep you contained within eyesight at all times. I hate these things, as if I needed one more obstacle to maneuver in the dead of night. Your poor knees are red and raw from crawling;

my poor knees are red and raw from slamming them into the wooden hurdles every 7 minutes. (I was never great at track in High School- and by "never great", I of course mean "never tried".)

In addition to crawling, you've now mastered the "pull-up", so I in turn have mastered the state of "constant fear". If you find something in your vicinity that happens to be a perfect head-smashing height, you feel the need to investigate what's sitting on top of it. You pull-up, start grunting and laughing in approval of your feat, then quickly start looking for the sharpest, hardest object below you that you feel the need to ram your face into.

You've been perfectly content during the last 9 months with the toys we've graciously bought to keep you entertained- until now. There are approximately 14 toys per square foot in this house, and yet you'll always manage to find the *one* object you're not supposed to have. Here are your favorite toys (and none of these are made up): every electrical outlet, the computer charger, any dog toy, the door stops, the Dish Network receiver, Mommy's shoes, any remote control, dog food, Plug-Ins, a rattlesnake covered in broken glass…(okay, maybe I made the *last* one up). I kid you not, I could fill the house thigh-high with kid's toys, throw in *one* kernel of the dog's food, and you would come up seconds later, gnawing away and drooling brown.

You're pretty much all baby food now. The bottles are saved for bedtime, or when mommy and daddy really need you to sleep for an hour. Formula has become your Dramamine. Your baby food is no longer of the simple one-ingredient nature like carrots or bananas. You've graduated to having a full course meal within the two ounce container- and they smell like it. It's now zucchini with peas and apples, or chicken and rice with mango. (I often wonder who sits around and decides what foods should go together. There's some weirdo in an office somewhere that thinks, "Hey, I know! How about broccoli and Vienna sausages in a white clam sauce?!")

I choose the food based merely on the activities of the day. If we're planning on venturing out into public, I go for the apples, pears, and bananas combo as it's a faint yellow in color. Your food still manages to find its way regurgitated onto your entire torso, so I save the green beans in brown gravy for when we're not leaving the house.

We have finally reached the blessed time when we can give you those little puff snacks. I tried one the first time. Not bad actually. They're pretty much just really soft pieces of cereal without any of color, sugar, or taste. These things are amazing- not because they provide a nutritious treat for you, but that they manage to keep you occupied for around 13 uninterrupted seconds at a time. We can spread these all over your highchair tray, and your engrossed long enough for mommy and daddy to eat over 4 bites of supper in a ROW- a feat that hasn't been seen since you were born.

I also love them because they provide daddy with hilarious entertainment. Since they're "Stage 1" snacks the pieces are about the size of a flea's earlobe, so it takes you a while to coordinate your finger and thumb to pick one up. Then you jam your entire fist into your mouth to devour the treat. The great part is that 90% of the time, you bring your fist out, and it's stuck to some other random part of your hand. You spend the next several minutes trying to track it down with your mouth, looking like your chasing an ant crawling around your fingers. By the end of the ordeal, you've actually eaten around 3 pieces and have 4 dozen stuck haphazardly around your body.

> *"It is admirable for a man to take his son fishing, but there is a special place in heaven for the father who takes his daughter shopping."*
> —John Sinor

PART 11

MY AUTUMN ANGEL

August 15, 2015

There have been countless posts in the last couple days about parents sending their innocent children off to their first day of school. I've enjoyed the countless pictures of little 5 year olds holding the sign stating "My first day in Kindergarten." What's great is that for every post of a child heading off to school, is one is usually immediately following with the parent expressing their fear, happiness, nervousness, and all the other emotions that tag along. You will be there soon, yourself, and I pray I have taught you well. I hope I have succeeded in teaching you right from wrong, how to live life correctly, how to love each other.

It really has been causing me to pause to think of our own father, and the relationship we each have with him, and him with us. For years he has tried desperately to teach *us* right from wrong, how to live life correctly, and love each other. But sometimes, we forget his instruction and the simplicity of his teaching.

There was once a young boy who was helping his father in the yard with some much-needed yard work. When the two unearthed a large rock, the father immediately saw the teaching opportunity. He told his son, "Okay, you see that rock? I need you to move it from there over to the woods."

Spurred on by the father's challenge, and never wanting to let him down, he began the task. He first tried lifting the rock, and quickly realized it was much too heavy for him. He went back to his father, and began to explain the impossibility of the mission he'd been given. "Son, have you tried everything? Have you exhausted all your resources?"

The young boy went at it again, trying everything he could imagine. Putting his back into it, trying to wedge it up with his shovel, everything. Tired, sweating, and defeated, he returned with his head low to his father, knowing full-well the disappointment from his dad would soon follow. "Son, are you sure you've tried everything?"

The tear-filled eyes gave his father his answer. But quickly came the reply, "No, you haven't. You have yet to ask me for my help." So many times when we're faced with the difficulties that are certain in our life, we immediately try everything on our own, and in my own experience, this usually ends with me failing, feeling defeated and ashamed in my father's presence. But, Punkin, before you give up. Before you throw in the towel, fold up the tent, go home and quit, remember this: He's always there for you. Simply stop for a minute, take a step back, look up at your Father's face, and say, "Hey Dad, I need some help." He'll gladly bend down, and help you with those large rocks.

> *"God is a safe place to hide,*
> *ready to help when we need him."*
> —Psalm 46:1

August 31, 2015

You're 10 months now, and have suddenly become somewhat of a brat. You know the way you like things to be done, and if they're not carried out exactly as Princess Punkin demands, you'll let us know. You will now bring your arm down, slapping your leg, and grunting, when you're mad about a particular event, scrunching up your nose as if to tell us you're disgusted about our choices.

So many fellow parents have said to me, "Oh, just wait until she *really* starts having the temper tantrums!" Not too concerned about those, because at least then I can spank your butt. Right now, if I smack your hand for trying to amputate the dog's ear, you look at me a laugh, as if I'm just beginning the daily Patty Cake lesson (no you still haven't learned it, and the doctor's going to end up holding Daddy back a grade).

As you've noticed, I haven't written in a couple weeks. We're desperately trying to sell this house, and have found a house we are prepared to buy as soon as this one sells. I've been working on packing, cleaning up the yard, getting finances in order, and working with the realtors. I've picked up extra shifts at work, and several more DJ jobs for weddings, so I could get more cash for all the new things I wanted. I've become so infatuated with the possibility of finally getting our dream home and all the junk to fill it that the month has quickly passed us by. In the few quiet moments we would spend together as a family in the evenings, I found myself shopping online for better furniture, bigger TV's, and ways to landscape the yard. You'd play in the floor by yourself until your 'tired' cry began, and I'd reluctantly put down the phone, so I could quickly put you to bed.

I essentially missed a whole month of your first year, and I'll never get that back. I was so blinded by my own dreams and desires, that you had taken a back burner. But at least I realized my error early in your life, and not long after you're already gone. I don't want you to grow up closer to your friends, toys, or TV's, than you are to your own Daddy.

MY AUTUMN ANGEL

The world has changed drastically over the course of a couple decades. Our views on happiness and how and what is used to achieve it has been thwarted. We spend our lives chasing the all mighty dollar, attempting to keep up with the Jones's, and displaying our goods as a show of our monetary and social status. And what is our reward for the gaining of these physical items of value? Shortened life spans, sickness, and health problems from lack of sleep, heightened stress levels, improper diet and worry. Little to no time spent with our families, and our children are suffering from lack of parental guidance. All too common these days, we see more and more families with both the Mother and Father working long hours, either in an attempt to make ends meet or to keep up with the current trends, and children growing up with babysitters of video games or television shows.

Children spend very little time outside; therefore they have lost touch with and respect for nature and wildlife. They have lost the ability to use their imaginations, and therefore have lost their innocents and the ability to think. They are not learning the moral and life lessons that are normally taught at home by Mom and Dad, and instead they are learning about morality and life via overcrowded classrooms and through videogames and TV programs. How do I hold you accountable for your actions when you're are not being taught basic morals by Dad at home? Telling you the rules is not the same as teaching you the rules (Give a man fish, feed him once; teach him to fish, feed him a lifetime).

As you've noticed, I have a tattoo in French down my arm that says, "Sometimes your dreams are what make you a slave." We try so hard to attain the right status, the nicest house, fastest car, perfect job, best clothes, that we find ourselves waking up at the end of our lives realizing that all these "dreams" have kept us from truly enjoying our lives on a daily basis. What are we really getting out of life if we spend so much time working to acquire things that we fail to enjoy what we have? A truly rich man is the one who is content, happy in the fact that he has all he requires and is in need of nothing. One who has everything his heart desires in that he has a family that loves him, a home to live in, food to nourish him and a place to worship.

So, I've spent the last couple days praising God for all the small things. The best parts of each day that I'll never have the chance to live again. The way you think it's hilarious to hold your feet when I'm trying to change your diaper. How you now start waving frantically at me if I get up to leave the room. The way your face lights up when I walk in the house after work. Your little feet, your infectious smile, your smell after a bath, when you laugh too much and end up with the hiccups.

If we get a bigger house, that's fine. If I have the chance to someday get a pool, that's great. If I'm finally able to get that projector so I can watch baseball on a 120 inch screen, that'd be awesome… But I'm not going to focus on all these "things" I don't have and be depressed, when I have all these amazing gifts in front of me already. You, your mommy, and Jesus are the only things I need, and if I can't find happiness in you three, then a pool definitely won't either.

September 3, 2015

You'll have plenty of instances in your life where you'll be asked, "Who do you consider your hero?" I've seen many people have to take several moments to ponder the question, but to me the answer has always been an immediate one. My father. If I turn out to be a great daddy to you, make sure to seek out your Papaw to thank him, because he taught me what it meant to be an amazing Dad.

When he was first married, he wrote a poem for your Mema, and after many more came. It was his way, much like I'm doing now, to express those feelings he had a hard him verbalizing. In August of 1977, when your Aunt Christy was little, he wrote one for her. I thought it fitting to share it with you as it's still relevant for Daddy-daughter relationships today, and I'm sure for many years to come.

MY AUTUMN ANGEL

"A Poem for Christy"

It's hard to believe
That you're growing so fast.
Soon having a "little girl"
Will be a thing of the past.

It seems such a short time
Since you were toddling around.
And it was really a struggle
Just to keep off the ground.

You were a dream come true
For your Mother and me,
And you've always been exactly
The way we'd hoped you would be.

I'm sorry for not spending
More time than I do.
Just doing the things
That you want me to do.

When you get down a toy
And say, "Daddy, let's play."
I usually tell you,
"Some other day."

Or you bring me a stack of books
At least a mile high,
But you know I won't read them
By the look in my eyes.

All the things that you love now
Will just grow more dear,
As they fade into memories
With each passing year.

As the years go by,
It makes me so blue.
Just to think how fast
Childhood will fly by for you.

I just hope when you're grown
And you speak of your Dad,
You'll tell about the good things
And good times we had.

I wish you all of the happiness
That this life has to give.
And remember, I'll love you
For as long as I live.

—R. Keith McDonald

September 8, 2015

I need you in my life, that's for sure. You've completely changed my attitude, my outlook, and my future. But you also need to understand how much you actually need me to. A good father has become a rare commodity in today's world, so never take that for granted, Punkin.

You need Daddy so that you'll always know what it's like to be somebody's favorite. You need me to answer all those tough questions that end up keeping you awake at night. You need me to prove that there are actually men in this world that can be trusted. You need me to help with school assignments when you're too tired to finish them yourself, to tuck you in and check under your bed for monsters, to protect you from lightning and thunder.

You need me to steer you down the right road, explain that not all boys are like the one that broke your heart, and to stand with you on your wedding day. You need me to teach you how peace always overcomes fear, that a loving family can endure anything, and how to continually focus your mind on the things in life that truly matter.

You need your Dad to fix your toys when they're broken, teach you how to stand up for yourself, explain the proper way to act like a lady, and to carry you when you're too tired to walk. You need me to redirect you when you begin veering in the wrong direction, to hold back your hair over the toilet when you're sick, and to hold you while you cry.

You need your Daddy to remind you that even if you're not the center of someone else's world, you'll always be the center of mine. You need me to be your hero, your inspiration, your comforter, your wisdom, mentor, counselor, and best friend. You need me to remind you how stunningly beautiful you truly are, that you'll never be too old to need me, and to keep a home that you'll always want to return to.

You need your Daddy so that you will never ever feel lonely. Simply close your eyes; I'll be right there.

MY AUTUMN ANGEL

> *"Daughter, be of good comfort;*
> *your faith has made you whole."*
> —Matthew 9:22

September 12, 2015

Having a father as an ER nurse has its ups and downs. On one hand, if a mosquito happens to sneeze in your general direction, I'm convinced you now have bird and swine black plague flu. On the other hand, your leg could fall off and I casually head to the bathroom to get you an ice pack. The latter has happened today.

You've been running a fever off and on for a few days, not eating or drinking, and crying incessantly. Your mother has begged to go to the hospital for a couple days now, but in all my medical knowledge, I knew it was nothing serious. Fast forward to present time, with you being admitted to the hospital for severe dehydration, strep, and an upper respiratory infection. Nice "medical knowledge" there Dad…

As I sat in the recliner holding you tonight, my heart was breaking. It wasn't breaking in fear or worry, just breaking because I knew the pain and discomfort you were in. Your mommy kept saying, "Aren't you worried about this?!" And I would continue to answer, "Nope, not at all." I knew you would be okay. You know how? I've seen this before. I've cared for countless little ones in your same position. I understood the symptoms and that it would take time for you to recover. I also understood that sickness can be a good thing for babies as it builds up your immune system so that your body may easily recognize and defeat that next sickness that comes knocking at your door. So, I just held you. I held you, played with your hair as you whimpered, tickled your back as you cried, and spoke repeatedly into your ear, "It's okay, Daddy's here."

God also knows. Someday, you will be struck down again. Sickness will threaten to weaken you, failures will try to break you, or a plummeting self-esteem may seem to incapacitate you. You may be trying to make those last few dollars stretch, you may be staring at a life of sin and regrets, or you may be feeling the overbearing weight of depression and heart-tearing sadness. But God truly does understand. He looks at your situation and thinks, "Yep, I've seen this before. I've seen this many many times before." I imagine the angels looking at your situation, and pleading with God, "Aren't you worried about this?" Hear him continually answer, "Nope, not at all."

He knows that as much as it breaks his heart to know you're hurting, you will be okay. He may not take this from you, but for good reason. This battle you're facing only builds up your spirit so that you may easily recognize and defeat that next battle that comes knocking at your door. So, in the meantime, simply lean into him and know he understands. Let him play with your hair as you whimper, and tickle your back as you cry. Hear him softly speak into your ear, "It's okay, Daddy's here."

September 15, 2015

While getting close to finishing up your first year, I asked a few dear friends to write me something on Fatherhood and raising children. A couple of their responses were too good not to share with you:

Titus Benton
Executive Director at The 25 Group;
Student Pastor at Current Christian Church;
Katy, TX

Put away your axes, dads. You won't need those here.

In his song, *Planting Trees,* Andrew Peterson poetically describes parenting:

> *"And many years from now, Long after we are gone,*
> *These trees will spread their branches out*
> *And bless the dawn."*

On good days, a dad is a tender, caring gardener. On bad days we are a grizzly, temperamental lumberjack. With a hasty swing of our axe we can suddenly sabotage the growth that has happened so slowly. What took years to nurture can be severely harmed – even destroyed – in an instant. I've seen it time and again as a student pastor.

Dad leaves. Dad lashes out. Dad limits.

A permanent impression is made on the daughter. Accidentally or on purpose, the dad has made his mark. Too many marks and the tree eventually falls over. It's serious stuff, this parenting. We must be cautious.

I asked my daughter to recall the nicest thing I've ever said or done for her. She searched her memory for a frontrunner, but couldn't deliver a specific instance. I then asked her what the meanest thing I said or worst thing I ever did for her was. She immediately remembered an occasion where my mouth outran my mind.

Hello, my name is Titus…and I'm a lumberjack.

As dads of little girls, it is important to remember that we should be in the business of planting trees, not chopping them down. We're growing something that will outlast us by more than mere longevity. Cared for properly, our daughters will out-live us as well – in love and in blessing and in justice. We're *planting* trees, not chopping them down.

Put away your axes dads. You won't need those here.

GAVIN McDONALD

Rich Key
Nashville, TN

All of my life I have been fascinated by girls. As a child, while all the other boys played sports, I was scouting out the prettiest girl and trying to make her like me. As I grew older, I noticed that every time I called a girl on the phone, talked to her at church, or went to her house, her dad always treated me like a serial killer. Although I was always intimidated as a child and even a young man, this never detoured my goal of getting the girl's attention.

As time went by and I grew older, my parents would continually say to me, "Son, we love you and pray for you and your wife every day." They never said girlfriend, always wife. When I met my wife, I knew immediately that she was the one God had intended for me to spend the rest of my life beside. Within a couple of years we married and started our life together. In June of 2007, we had our first child; a baby boy, and couldn't have been happier. All I could think of was hunting, fishing, and bringing him up to be a strong Godly man. Three and a half years later, we discovered that we would be having another child and it would be a little girl. Now, this is where my story really begins.

Since the second she was born, there was something different. When I had my son, my thoughts were that I couldn't wait to get him his first motorcycle or take him on the ski boat as fast as it would go while he was tubing behind me; all the stupid dangerous stuff my dad and I did. But with her, there was something different. From day one, I was her protector and we had a different kind of bond. I loved her just as much as my son, but felt like she needed more protection from the world.

As my little girl began to age, I began to think back when I was a little boy and remembered the only things boys usually think about – girls. This began to make me hate little boys. I started having dreams about prom, dates, movies, holding hands and all kinds of other crazy stuff. My wife always thought this was funny, but I never found the humor in it. I would tell her things that I planned on doing in the future – like when she goes on her first date when she's 30. I imagine myself standing at the door with a long beard, tattoos to my fingertips, looking crazy and holding a shotgun, letting him know if she's not home by 9:00 I'm coming for him. I began to understand why all of those dads had that look in their eyes. They didn't hate me; they simply hated seeing their baby girl venture into the time of life where so many mistakes began to happen.

Although my daughter is not old enough to date yet, I know that inevitable day is coming. My mind goes back to my Mom and Dad saying over and over, "Son, we love you and pray for you and your wife every day." Today I am married to the woman of my dreams and she is amazing in every way. This was no coincidence; it was prayer. As parents, we need to pray for our children and their spouses often. Pray that God gives our children wisdom to make the Godly decisions when the time comes. If you want your children to have a healthy marriage, show them through example. If you want your children to have a Godly marriage, show them through example.

The Bible tells us in Jeremiah 1:5, " "Before I formed you in the womb I knew you, before you were born I set you apart; I appointed you as a prophet to the nations." Pray for your daughters and their spouse now. Love them and pray for God's guidance in their lives. If you do this, you may never even need to use the shotgun.

Ray Perkins
Kansas City, MO

I have two daughters and three boys, but my youngest daughter, Nkauj Yeeb Yinora Lee Perkins (yes, it's a mouthful!), is my payback, as she's just like me. All I can do is inspire fathers to be the best encourager in our daughter's lives; a life that is constantly saturated with reality TV's views of false beauty. As fathers, we need to let our daughter's know that they're beautiful every day and in every way. Be their best examples of gentleness, kindness and a higher standard of morals. We can't expect our daughters to marry their king, if we don't first raise them as a queen.

Joshua Shaw
Mount Vernon, OH

I've always been a guy who has loved "big", and when I became a father in 2011, I thought it would be the same. I knew the type of love I had for family and friends and the type of love that has grown over the years for my bride. Even with being a pastor for nearly fifteen years, I thought I had this love thing figured out. When my daughter Willow was born, I thought my love for her would fit in either of those categories; however, I was completely wrong. When I first held her, a part of my heart and spirit opened up that I never knew existed, and I was filled with a love I have never experienced before; a father's love.

These past four years of being a Dad has given me a microscopic glimpse into a love that our Heavenly Father has for us: a love that is unconditional and never-ending. Becoming a father has helped me strengthen my relationships with those around me, has given me a deeper understanding of what it is to be "man", and how to better reciprocate the love Christ has expressed to me.

Shawn Sanseverino
Associate Pastor, The Grace Place Church
Arlington, TX

Have you ever been praying for your family and children and said the common phrase, "I pray that you put a hedge of protection around my family?"

I have prayed this over my family many times during the last fourteen years. It was spring-time in 2012, and my daughter was about one year old. This was such a beautiful phase of life, and I would often put her to sleep on my shoulder as I walked around my house and prayed. This particular morning, I began the same opening prayer I had prayed for many years, but for some reason this time God talked back to me as I held my little girl.

God showed me in my mind's eye the picture of a hedge. It was really simple: imagine you are standing with a parking lot off in the distance, and you see a hedge of shrubs surrounding a parking lot. The hedge was broken up in a few places around the parking lot because of heavy foot traffic, which eventually created a clear path for the unwanted guest to easily breach the hedge when needed.

God asked me, "What do you see?"

Well God, I see the shrubs placed as a hedge of protection marking the boundaries of that parking lot. It's as if they are used as a boundary marker for keeping unwanted traffic and activity flowing in and out.

God spoke back to me and said, "Yes, you're right, that hedge is for keeping out unwanted company."

I had these instant thoughts flood my heart as God was speaking to me. I remember writing down in my journal, "You were saved into the Family of God and have been made in the image of God. Just like Adam was designed to rule and take authority in the garden, my design for mankind is the same. You were created to rule and take authority as my Son."

I remember one specific time when I went to a restaurant and parked on the wrong side of the lot. I was actually not in the right parking lot at all. As I walked toward the restaurant, there were hedges surrounding the parking of the restaurant and I could not get over. The hedges were a little too tall for me to climb or jump over, so I began to walk around the hedge looking for a way through. All of the sudden, I noticed a "Break in the Hedge" and a nice little beaten path where others had snuck through. I joyfully and easily walked through to enjoy a nice lunch.

And there was my revelation. God said, "Shawn, you have more authority than you know. You are asking me to put a hedge of protection around your home, but I made *you* the head of your home, and I have placed you as a hedge for your household. You are the priest of your home, so take the authority I have given you. You do this by the way you live, and when you leave cracks for unwanted guests in your own life, you are simultaneously leaving cracks for unwanted guests in the life of your family, your kids, your daughter."

Dad's broken hedges are created by character flaws, passed down generational dysfunctions, sin, discord, and everything else that saddens the heart of our God. As you and I tolerate these things in our home they become open paths in the hedge of protection around our family. These open paths in our hedge create a clearly marked out path for the enemy to happily walk through and reap havoc in your life.

As it was told to Adam while he was in the Garden in Genesis 1, "Subdue the earth, take dominion, and take authority."

Dads please hear me; you have more authority than you know! How we live our lives as men of God from a day to day basis determines how well our hedge protects our family.

What does that hedge around your home look like? Are there breaks in the hedge with a nice clear path for the enemy to travel through whenever he wants?

There was a time as a young man when I did not serve the Lord. The hedge that surrounded me was mangled and broken by my own doing, and some of the breaks were passed down from my father. Yours is most likely similar. We must remember that a steady dose of God's Word at work in our life combined with our submission to His Word is always enough to sustain us. It is God's grace in us that enables us to live a life that is honorable to him. A life submitted to the Lord is the kind that breads a healthy spiritual environment in our homes. Unfortunately, there is no other way to protect our families. There are no amounts of gifts, family vacations, or entertainment that can protect and provide for your family like you.

Take the authority that has been given to us to protect and provide for our daughters the way the Lord has designed us to. Continually walk the parameter of your heart; checking for signs of illegal entry and breaks in your hedge. You will find that more you pray, the more that thin shrub barrier turns into a tall fortified wall.

October 16, 2015

A young girl was walking home from school one day when she came across a group of older girls. These were the dreaded 6th graders that no little 2nd grader would ever dare to cross. They were the rough ones, the mean ones, the fighters, the bruisers. She had no milk money to fork over, and nothing of value to surrender to the gang, so she knew what would come next. They began to beat her. Knocking her books out of her hand, pulling her hair, they proceeded to punish her for being young, for being a dork, for not fitting in, for not being pretty enough, and well…pretty much for her just being her.

She didn't deserve it. That's when, while lying in the dust with her broken pride lying next to her, she looked up and noticed her dad standing on the other side of the playground, watching. And it sparked something in the little girl. She began to fight back. Digging deep into her spirit, she began to overcome the bullies. She began to win. The group of 6th graders quickly ran away, and the little girl limped to her father's side.

What happened here? What changed when she saw her father? Simply this: she knew that her father would never stand back and allow her to go through something that he didn't think she could handle. The father knows the daughter better than anyone. He knows what's too much. He knows what will break her. But he also knows the battles, even though they may be painful, are many times quite essential to shape the young woman into a champion.

So many times in your life, while slap in the middle of pain and hurt, you'll wonder where your God is. Painful blow after painful blow, you'll lie in the dust and wonder when he's planning on coming to your rescue. That's when you look up and see him watching you; eye's wide with hope and determination, knowing that you are capable of succeeding. You'll see his lips whisper, "You can do this, Kinley. Come on, you can do this…"

And you know what? He's right. You can. Refuse to be paralyzed by my problem, and instead decide to be persuaded by his promise. The promise in his word that says he will never give you more than you can handle. And the next time you come across a tough group of 6th graders, simply remember that your father isn't too far away, ready to tag in if needed.

October 19, 2015

The statement I've heard the most over the last year is to enjoy the moment as it flies by so fast. I remember thinking, "When is she ever going to sit up by herself?" I blink, and it's happened. Then, "It's taking her forever to crawl" I turn around, and it's happened. And now, you're walking. I took a breath, and it happened.

Well, I say walking, but it's more like seeing a baby deer on wet ice the majority of the time. Your hands and arms flail about as you constantly try to keep balance, your eyes deadest on some inanimate object you're obviously not supposed to have. With the new walking feat, you've now become insanely quick. At times, I wish you left a rainbow-like snail trail behind you so that finding you would be easier.

Your new favorite place is the bathroom, as you've learned how to open drawers. You found this out the other day when daddy had to bring you with him to "take care of some business". Within 3 seconds of me sitting down, you'd pulled out all the supplies necessary to successfully de-clog the shower drain, which I found hilarious only due to the fact that your crack was hanging out the top of your diaper like a true plumber. Maybe you've found your calling.

The hardest challenge over the last few weeks has been to remove all objects from your mouth you've randomly found on the floor in your journeys. If I ever notice that you've stopped moving for a few consecutive seconds, you're either pooping or chewing relentlessly on something forbidden. A small sample of things I've finger-swept out of your mouth: a tack, several Altoids, a nail clipping, a nickel, a Walmart receipt, a bobby pin, a packing peanut, a candy wrapper, a pen cap, a leaf, and multiple dog treats that Evie had hidden…obviously not very well. I'm shocked your diapers don't look like the kitchen junk drawer. I keep checking them for that white watch I misplaced. You got hold of the outlet plug-in yesterday, and were gulping the liquid before I could rush over to you. You lost your mind and cried for an hour, but at least you smelled like a harvest sunset for a couple days.

You have now realized that when I reach for something you have, you can move your hand away quickly, which allows for a few more seconds with the acquired object while daddy regroups. It always makes me look like a moron, and imagine myself looking like a cat chasing a laser light, grasping at air for way too long, while knowing I'm being outsmarted by an 11 month old.

The dining room has been converted into the party planning headquarters. I've never seen so much fabric, glitter, candy, and spray-painted crafts in one place before. It's safe to say we may have gone a little overboard. I've had pink and gold paint under my nails now for a month. We've rented a banquet hall at the local recreation club, and that's only because it would cost too much to fly all the family over to the Taj Mahal – mommy's first choice of venue. It's a bad sign when the FedEx driver knows your whole family by name, and I've actually even considered sending him an invitation, seeing as he's practically watched you grow up.

Everyone keeps saying, "Why are you spending so much time and energy on something she'll never remember?" Well, because it's a celebration of your birth! Okay, that's a lie. I'm actually throwing the party to honor myself in achieving the feat of keeping you alive for 12 straight months – never thought I'd make it. Yep, I've definitely earned this party.

October 21, 2015

As I sit in the house with you while Mommy works, these 12 hours can easily feel like 12 days. So I'm constantly trying to find things to fill my time. I ran with you to the store in an attempt to come across something that might help quicken the time trapped at home, and I seriously considered buying a puzzle that I saw for sale.

You've seen the type: eagle flying over Mount Rushmore with the American flag in its talons. It was hideous, but in a weird way, enticing. I was then reminded of my utter hatred for puzzles. I can never finish one. Ever. I'm way too high-strung and ADHD to put the time and effort into actually making it past finding all the sides. So, I instead bought you one. This *may* be a puzzle that I'll be able to handle – seeing as it has 6 pieces…and they're all sides.

You were excited to have a new toy, but quickly became frustrated when the pieces didn't fit quite like you wanted them to. You became disinterested and I personally feel your pain, seeing as the tedious task of attempting to fit all the different shapes together to produce a picture is daunting. I can recall only once when I completed a very large puzzle. It was nothing but hundreds of different salt and pepper shakers. When I placed the last piece, I sat back, exhaled deeply, and took in the glorious picture. I was so proud of my accomplishment, I even had mom buy the glaze to paint over it, so that it may remain intact for eternity.

It's an unforgettable feeling to see all the pieces fit together perfectly. Wouldn't it be great if we also saw this in life? But so many times, it never quite goes as smoothly. We end up with pieces that never seem to fit where you think they should, various holes throughout your picture, or even pieces you've misplaced somewhere along the way.

There have been countless times that I've looked at a puzzle piece all by itself, swearing that it didn't belong in *my* puzzle. "Wait, this heartbreak doesn't fit here." But sure enough, the piece eventually finds its place, and it is not until we see the entire picture that we understand its role. Sweetie, there will be many pieces of your life that you will look at with uncertainty, and question God as to its rightful place in your story. Can you imagine if I picked up the phone on some Saturday morning, called Bob Ross while I'm watching his painting show, and said, "Umm, I'm pretty sure you put that pretty little tree in this picture by mistake." May I make a suggestion? Don't question the artist of the picture before you see the final work.

If you ever find yourself swimming in a sea of heart-ache, always remember those times are not corner pieces, they're simply connectors. It's not something you're building your final picture around; it's simply a filler until you understand the full picture. If it wasn't for all those middle, connecting, seemingly meaningless pieces, your picture would definitely not be worth God finally glazing and framing the finished product.

"For it is God who is at work in you, both to will and to work for His good pleasure."
—Philippians 2:13

October 31, 2015

I've been a father for a year now. Over that time I've spent hundreds of hours sitting at this computer trying to set some sort of foundation that you can build on for your life. I've tried to inspire, encourage, and train. One thing I haven't done is step back for a moment to explain what you've done for *me*. So here it goes:

You've taught me that this world was not set into motion on my account. It's not about me. Everything I do now revolves around your happiness and success.

You have stripped away everything that was dying in my life, and began to water all the small good things that I had pushed deep down inside. I'd turned into a cynic; you've brought me into compassion. I'd become a dead end; you showed me a new road. I've come to rely on only myself; you've taught me that wisdom comes from God. I had come to love myself only; you've shown me the greatest thing in the world is when you love someone else.

Before you, nothing mattered anymore. I worked to pay bills, I ate to stay alive, and I slept because I was bored. Life was meaningless and tedious. You changed everything. I now come home simply to see your smile. I work to give you the world. I get up in the morning to hold you. I sit for hours to simply stare into your eyes. I live to watch you live.

I chose the title "Raise Her Up", because when you were born I realized that you would learn how to live by watching me. If I didn't raise you up to honor and serve God, then I could lose you forever. We have only a few short years to spend together on this Earth, but if I raise you up right, we'll get to spend eternity together.

In this, you saved my life. In realizing how I should raise you, I recommitted myself to God. The first night home, I knelt by your crib and cried out for forgiveness. With tears streaming down my face, I placed my hands on your head and prayed. I prayed with every fiber of my being that I would become the father you needed and the father that

God required. I felt the weight of responsibility for you placed upon my shoulders. My relationship with our heavenly father truly began the day I became your daddy. For the first time in my life, I got a small taste of what I imagine God feels for us. You're constantly on my mind, you're always in my prayers, and I want to give you the world…so does God. But the awesome thing is that someday, he actually will.

Before I met you, I never realized what it was like to look at someone and smile for no reason. Before you were conceived, I wanted you. Before you were born, I loved you. Before you were here an hour, I would die for you. You brought back my joy. You brought back my happiness. You didn't just make me come out of the shadows – you helped pull away everything that was blocking the sun. You are my greatest adventure. Being a father is the best thing I've ever experienced, and because of you, I now have a small glimpse of the unrelenting and undying love of God.

"I'll love you forever. I'll like you for always. As long as I'm living, my baby you'll be."
—Robert Munsch

PART 12

CLOSING

I bought a lottery ticket today. Don't ask me why, as this is something I rarely do, but for some unknown reason I spontaneously wanted to play the odds. Shockingly, I lost. As I was driving home I was mad at myself for wasting the 5 dollars, and thinking about all the misfortune of my life. It seems I've found myself on the odd end of the odds countless times in my 33 years.

Then I thought of you, as I do constantly. I remember a year ago, sitting in a doctor's office and feeling my throat tighten with fear. My ears heard the words, "We are not sure what's going to happen. We are not hopeful that the stitch will hold. We are playing against the odds."

I have told you many things over the last 12 months, but let me leave you with this: God loves it when the odds are against him. He doesn't like it when everything is in his favor, because when it's *not* against the odds and you come out on top, nobody takes notice. God isn't going to do something that's just mediocre, he's going to step into a situation where he knows when people see it, and they will *know* it was because of him. Let me prove it to you:

God used a stuttering man to go to the most powerful nation in the world, look up at them and say, "Let my people go!" Why? Why, when God needed a mouthpiece, did he send a stuttering Moe with a beard down to his knees? He doesn't like it when the odds are in his favor.

CLOSING

When Gideon was preparing for battle with his 33,000 men, God looked down and said, "Whoa, that's *way* too many people! We're going to have to trim that down a little bit!" When 300 men were left standing with Gideon, God said, "That's much better! Now, the odds are *really* against us!" He doesn't like it when the odds are in his favor.

God used an itty-bitty boy that nobody had noticed to pluck out of the mountains where he was watching his sheep, and placed him in front of a giant that *everyone* had noticed! He could have used anyone! He could have chosen some mighty warrior, but instead chose a pee-on. He doesn't like it when the odds are in his favor.

Jesus was sitting on a hillside with 5,000 hungry men with only 5 loaves of bread and two fish. Odds are, everyone's going to remain hungry. Lazarus wasn't just dead, he was stinking by now- spending the last 4 days in a tomb. Odds are, Lazarus wasn't going anywhere. A man came stumbling to Jesus saying he's been blind since birth. Odds are, he is never going to see. But...he doesn't like it when the odds are in his favor.

Last September, we were told if everything went well it would be a phenomenon, and God's ears perked up. The doctors said it would be a miracle, and God leaned in closer to listen. Everyone was telling us that the odds were against us, and that's when God jumped up, cracked his knuckles, and went to work.

You are our miracle, because God wanted to show up and show off. You must always remember, for the rest of your life, that God looks forward to flipping the odds in your favor.

I have no idea what you will face in the next 10, 30, or 50 years. I don't know what heartache, sickness, trouble, or circumstances may try to break your spirit. But listen: you are serving a God that cancer doesn't make him nervous, depression doesn't make him nervous, financial problems don't make him nervous.

Life is short, and the odds are that when we die, we die and that's it. Take all that I've taught you in the last year, and live by these words.

GAVIN McDONALD

If you do, once again God will beat the odds, and we'll get to spend eternity together, having more fun than we could ever imagine. I hope they have Candy Land. Candy Land is my jam.

I'll love you forever, Punkin.
—Daddy

Note from the Publisher

Are you a first time author?

Not sure how to proceed to get your book published?
Want to keep all your rights and all your royalties?
Want it to look as good as a Top 10 publisher?
Need help with editing, layout, cover design?
Want it out there selling in 90 days or less?

Visit our website for some exciting new options!

www.chalfant-eckert-publishing.com

www.ingramcontent.com/pod-product-compliance
Lightning Source LLC
Chambersburg PA
CBHW052032070526
44584CB00016B/2006